Tyrannus Rex

A Field Guide to Countering Modern Tyranny

Tyrannus Rex

A Field Guide to Countering Modern Tyranny

E.A. Blair

BURN BAG PRESS

Tyrannus Rex: A Field Guide to Countering Modern Tyranny

Contact: info@burnbagpress.com

ISBN: 979-8-9954425-0-9

First Edition

This book is a work of political analysis and civic education. It synthesizes historical research, political science, and psychology to document authoritarian tactics and evidence-based resistance strategies. The content is intended for educational purposes and reflects the author's analysis of historical and contemporary political systems.

The examples cited reflect historical events and recurring patterns of authoritarian behavior documented across multiple regimes and time periods. The tactics and behaviors described are archetypal patterns, observed across different leaders, parties, and nations. Readers may recognize these patterns in contemporary contexts; such recognition reflects the universality of authoritarian methods, not commentary on specific individuals. Illustrations are allegorical representations of political archetypes and structural dynamics, not depictions of specific persons or entities.

Nothing in this text constitutes legal advice. All recommendations for civic action are grounded in principles of nonviolent resistance and assume operation within legal frameworks. Where countermeasures are described in the context of advanced authoritarian conditions, they reflect historically documented responses to the erosion or weaponization of those frameworks, not encouragement to circumvent legitimate law enforcement. Readers are responsible for understanding applicable laws in their jurisdictions.

While every effort has been made to ensure accuracy, readers should verify information independently and consult appropriate professionals before taking action.

for Gary

You shall know the truth,
and the truth shall set you free.

—John 8:32

Table of Contents

Table of Contents CONTINUED

Table of Contents CONTINUED

Table of Contents CONTINUED

Table of Contents CONTINUED

Introduction

If you are reading this book, darkness has likely already begun to fall. You may live in an authoritarian state where freedom has faded into memory, or in a democracy where the gears of self-government are beginning to grind in reverse. You feel anger, unease, and a growing sense of powerlessness. You want to act, but are unsure about what to do.

This book is written for you.

It is a synthesis of three distinct areas of study: the history of how tyrannical regimes rise and fall; the political science of what makes resistance movements succeed or fail; and the psychology of the authoritarian mind. The goal is to distill this research into concrete lessons of resistance available to ordinary citizens navigating extraordinary times.

Central to this approach is the concept of prebunking. Research on misinformation demonstrates that the most effective countermeasure is often the simplest: revealing how the trick is performed. Just as a vaccine inoculates the body by exposing it to a weakened pathogen, understanding the mechanics of manipulation inoculates the mind against deception. This book is designed to provide that immunity, equipping you to see through the lies and propaganda and know the truth.

Consider this the first lesson: vaccines rely on herd immunity, and so does truth.

Tyranny thrives in isolation, severing connections to make individuals feel powerless and alone. Therefore, resistance is not a solitary act. When you learn these mechanics, you protect your own mind; when you expose them to friends, family, and your community, you protect theirs. You resist by stripping the lies of their power before they can take root in your mind and the minds of those around you. To do this effectively, you must come to know the enemy.

This brings us to the second lesson: kings and tyrants are not the same thing.

History is littered with kings who were not tyrants, rulers who held absolute power but wielded it with a sense of duty or restraint. And the world is equally full of tyrants who are never kings, petty despots in boardrooms and HOAs who possess the pathology of control but lack the apparatus of the state.

But occasionally, history deals a fatal hand. The absolute authority of the sovereign intersects with the malignant pathologies of power.

We call this convergence *Tyrannus Rex*: The Tyrant King.

The principal danger lies in their disguise. Biologically, the Tyrant King is a typical human. They smile, they speak, they bleed. But, psychologically, they are a different species. They do not perceive the world as a network of social contracts, shared empathy, or mutual obligations. They see only a vertical hierarchy of predators and prey, dominance and submission. To understand them—and ultimately, to survive them—you must stop projecting your own humanity onto them. You must learn to see the creature beneath the crown.

But learning to see them is only the beginning.

To defeat a Tyrant King, you must understand the mechanics of their madness. You cannot fight what you cannot name, and you cannot survive a predator whose hunting patterns remain a mystery. We will strip away the camouflage, dissecting the predictable rhythms of their behavior, from the chaotic compulsions used to distract the public to the state terrors used to crush it.

For every tactic employed by the tyrant, there are countermeasures available to the ordinary citizen. While these individual acts of defiance may seem insignificant in isolation, when exercised at scale, they become a seismic force capable of felling even the most entrenched regime. We will explore how to build parallel structures of truth in a landscape of lies, how to starve the spectacle of its power, and how to create the friction necessary to slow the gears of oppression. The objective is not merely to endure the darkness. It is to empower you with the clarity and the tools to manage the fear, outlast the regime, and ultimately, reclaim your freedom.

When Benjamin Franklin left the Constitutional Convention in 1787, a bystander asked him what kind of government the delegates had created. "A republic," he replied, "if you can keep it." Franklin knew that self-government is a fragile achievement, one that survives only through the vigilance and virtue of its citizens. His warning applies to every society that aspires to govern itself. This book is written in that spirit: to help citizens everywhere recognize the forces that threaten self-rule, and to arm them with the knowledge to defend it.

STAGE I

The Pathologies of Power

Every authoritarian regime begins as a delusion in the mind of a single individual. Before the laws change, before the prisons fill, we witness the incubation of the *Tyrannus Rex*. The creature is defined by a specific cluster of pathologies that prime it with a relentless instinct for dominion. While considered defects in a healthy psyche, these traits function as evolutionary advantages in the pursuit of authority, stripping away moral inhibitions and equipping the aspirant with the ruthless tendencies required for ascent. Whether infiltrating a political party or a government bureau, it rises through the ranks by exploiting trust and neutralizing rivals. Yet, at this stage, its reach is still limited by its immediate orbit; it is a monster-in-the-making searching for the machinery to amplify its will. While no single leader exhibits every symptom, and the severity varies by case, the diagnostic patterns are unmistakable. To outmaneuver this predator, we must wield the capacity it lacks: empathy. Drawing from the profiles of tyrant kings past and present, we isolate ten defining traits to find the cracks in the armor. We study the compulsions. We inhabit its instincts. We map the pathology to ultimately render it extinct.

IN THIS STAGE

Chaos Compulsion • Edifice Complex • Grandiosity
Impunity Instinct • Machiavellianism • Malignant Narcissism
Messianic Complex • Predatory Kinship • Psychopathy • Sadism

IT WAS
GETTING
TOO QUIET.
AGAIN!?

Chaos Compulsion

DEFINITION

Chaos Compulsion is the authoritarian's pathological intolerance of stability, driven by an unthinking, addictive need for high-intensity stimulation. To this personality, often conditioned by a history of instability or neurodivergent traits, routine is viscerally unbearable. The leader instinctively creates crisis as a mechanism to distract from deep-seated internal anxiety, paradoxically generating external stress to soothe their own inner turmoil. Finding a perverse sense of focus and "normalcy" only within the eye of a storm, they drive a repetitive, addiction-like cycle of firing officials, provoking conflicts, and reversing policies to ensure the leader remains the emotional center of gravity while exhausting the people and institutions around them.

EXAMPLE

A leader cycles endlessly from one crisis to the next, ensuring the news cycle never settles. Cabinet members are praised one day and publicly humiliated or dismissed the next, reinforcing fear and personal dependence. Alliances are abandoned, policies reversed, and norms shattered through impulsive announcements or late-night decrees. Manufactured threats dominate headlines, while long-term governance and infrastructure quietly decays. Supporters perceive the volatility as necessary disruption, insisting that instability is proof of progress. Critics, overwhelmed by constant outrage, struggle to sustain focus or accountability. Over time, the nation becomes trapped in a permanent state of chaos, where the only constant is the leader's insatiable need for attention.

TELLTALE SIGNS OF CHAOS COMPULSION

Management by Chaos

The regime is marked by a relentless, illogical churning of personnel. The leader fires or humiliates even their most loyal lieutenants, often without clear cause. This prevents any subordinate from accumulating the institutional knowledge or influence to become a rival. By keeping the inner circle in a state of terror and flux, the only stable fixture is the leader.

Policy Whiplash

The leader frequently issues contradictory orders or reverses settled positions within the same news cycle. This "whiplash" is a control mechanism: by destroying the predictive capacity of the law and the bureaucracy, they force the entire state to freeze and wait for their specific command. This breaks the reliance on rules and trains the system to rely entirely on the leader's momentary whim.

An Allergy to Stability

The leader displays a distinct psychological intolerance for quiet governance or steady progress. Whenever the political landscape quiets or the news cycle drifts away from them, they instinctively invent a crisis to seize the narrative back. They start "fires" so they can be seen holding the hose.

CITIZEN COUNTERMEASURES

Ignoring the Provocations

Maintaining a disciplined silence regarding daily provocations prevents the leader from monopolizing the public's cognitive bandwidth. Instead of reacting to every inflammatory statement, small community groups focus resources on documenting a single, persistent failure, such as local infrastructure decay. By refusing to amplify the regime's "noise," citizens provide a stable informational anchor that breaks the cycle of distraction and preserves collective focus.

Highlighting Broken Promises

Pairing historical footage of the leader's past promises with current images of systemic failure produces a "shareable contradiction" for social media. By focusing on a single issue, such as rising food prices or unfinished roads, individuals bypass the need for complex explanations. This simplified visual evidence forces the leader's volatility into the public's daily awareness, rendering their distractions ineffective against the weight of lived reality.

Following the "Not My Circus" Rule

Withholding the voluntary labor often used to "fix" state dysfunction ensures the leader's incompetence remains visible. When citizens stop navigating around bureaucratic breakdowns and instead allow administrative errors to impact the system as intended, the chaos remains localized at the regime's doorstep. This tactical withdrawal of civic ingenuity prevents the leader from using a functional society to mask a dysfunctional government.

FOR THE ANIMALS
MY NAME IS
NAPOLEON,
KING OF KINGS:
LOOK ON MY WORKS,
YE MIGHTY,
AND DESPAIR!

Edifice Complex

DEFINITION

An Edifice Complex is the authoritarian impulse to construct monumental structures or annex territory to project power and glory. These spectacles of stone and soil are propaganda in physical form, casting the leader as a visionary, the nation as flourishing, and the regime as timeless. The phenomenon reflects a narcissistic need to convert political insecurity into historical permanency, often manifesting when a dictator feels their grip slipping. By favoring brutalist aesthetics and overwhelming scale, these structures are designed to make ordinary citizens feel insignificant against the might of the state. Ultimately, they represent a desperate bid for immortality, prioritizing concrete legacies over human welfare while draining the national treasury.

EXAMPLE

An authoritarian faces growing unrest and a collapsing economy. To reassert control, they announce a "national renewal" initiative to symbolize unity and progress. The project is unveiled with patriotic fanfare: a thousand-room palace, a mile-high tower, and a new capital city allegedly "for the people." Construction begins at breakneck speed, often demolishing legacy neighborhoods and cultural heritage sites to rewrite the nation's history. Contracts are funneled to regime loyalists while the treasury bleeds, creating a kleptocratic ecosystem disguised as urban planning. When critics question the astronomical cost, the leader denounces them as foreign agents or traitors who "hate their own country," turning the architecture itself into a loyalty test.

TELLTALE SIGNS OF EDIFICE COMPLEX

Extravagance Amid Hardship

The projects are symbolic gestures of power, not practical solutions to public problems. A leader will pour billions into a new "Palace of Culture" or a colossal stadium while the nation's basic infrastructure crumbles from underfunding. The goal is to create the illusion of progress and modernity rather than actually delivering it.

The Fixation on "Historical" Borders

This complex eventually outgrows the capital city. The leader begins to view the national map as a floor plan that is "incomplete." They obsess over reclaiming "lost" territory or "reunifying" populations, declaring their invasions as necessary steps to restore the nation's true, imperial glory.

Monuments to the Leader, Not the People

The projects are defined by their intimidating, monumental scale. This architectural style is subconsciously favored to aggrandize the leader and dwarf the ordinary citizen. Vast plazas, towering facades, and massive, block-like structures are designed to make people feel small and powerless, while the state appears permanent and all-powerful.

CITIZEN COUNTERMEASURES

Checking the Price Tag

Recasting the spectacle from a symbol of pride to a sign of corruption disrupts the intended narrative. Tracing the debt and revealing the beneficiaries shifts the focus to the opportunity cost. Juxtaposing images of opulent monuments with collapsing infrastructure creates a "visual audit" of the regime's priorities. This contrast effectively drains the project of its grandeur, revealing it as a vanity project and theft of public resources.

Raising the Cost of Collaboration

Prestige projects often rely on risk-averse international firms for design and construction. By issuing formal notices of future liability to architects, engineers, and insurers, activists signal that collaboration carries the threat of future criminal or civil prosecution. Coupling this with administrative roadblocks, such as zoning appeals, environmental challenges, and labor disputes, creates procedural gridlock. This friction raises the "compliance cost" until partners withdraw, leaving the monument unbuilt.

Reclaiming Civic Space

Denying the leader immortality requires repurposing edifices into public assets and returning annexed territories to their rightful sovereigns. A palace becomes a soup kitchen or a museum. Conquered land is returned to its people. When repurposing is not possible, the answer is simpler and more final. Demolition denies the leader their monument. Reparations deny them their conquest.

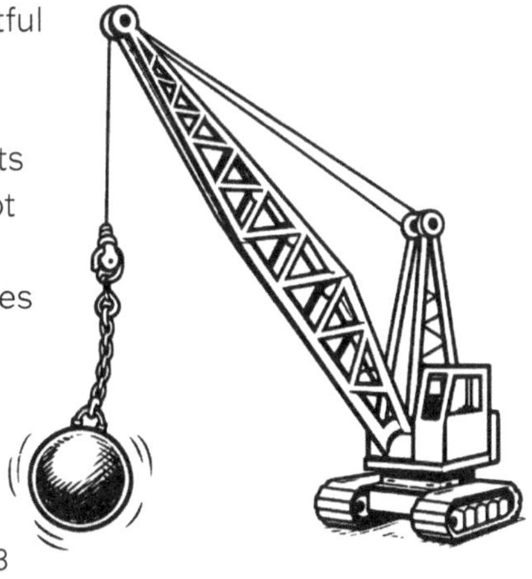

NEXT.

Grandiosity

DEFINITION

Grandiosity serves as a compensatory shield, masking deep-seated feelings of inferiority. Unlike genuine self-assurance, this display is a defense mechanism designed to protect a fragile core from the pain of a damaged self-image. It is often linked to vulnerable or covert narcissism, a variant in which the grandiosity runs beneath the surface rather than announcing itself openly. In either form, the pathology manifests as a relentless performance of perfectionism, entitlement, and inflated achievement, where even minor criticisms trigger intense, disproportionate reactions. The craving for constant praise inevitably yields diminishing returns, deepening the underlying insecurity and forcing the individual into ever-more desperate cycles of public dominance to ward off inadequacy. The pursuit of validation is endless, and no amount of praise can fill the void that drives it.

EXAMPLE

A leader obsessively tracks rankings, crowd sizes, and accolades, publicly measuring success by visibility and praise. Every prestigious award or mark of distinction is pursued as personal validation. Sensing this need, organizations and foreign governments quickly learn to offer up shiny honorifics to gain favor. When authentic recognition fails to materialize, the leader attacks the awarding bodies as corrupt, while loyal media insist the honor was politicized. Diplomatic efforts are recast as résumé-building exercises, and policy is shaped to maximize personal credit. The state becomes a stage for self-celebration, and national interest is subordinated to the leader's need for validation.

TELLTALE SIGNS OF GRANDIOSITY

Fabrication of Alternative Status Hierarchies

When mainstream institutions refuse to grant the desired prestige, the regime establishes counterfeit equivalents. The leader creates new awards, hall-of-fame inductees, or media rankings where their supremacy is guaranteed. By building a closed ecosystem of praise populated by sycophants and state-run entities, the leader constructs an alternate reality of illusory respect and success.

Commoditization of Honors

The leader treats awards, academic degrees, and military ranks as props to support a fragile self-image. There is a persistent pattern of courting universities, media outlets, and civic organizations to extract titles or glowing coverage. Whether status markers are collected or earned, they serve as psychological armor to fend off feelings of inadequacy.

Retaliatory Grievance Against Arbiters

Institutions that withhold validation are punished. When awards and cultural accolades are denied, the response is immediate and coordinated: a public attack on the granting body's legitimacy. The institution is not simply wrong. It is corrupt and foreign-influenced. By claiming every rejection is evidence of a rigged system, the leader accomplishes something strategically elegant: personal disappointment is converted into political grievance, and any standard of excellence the leader cannot meet is simply declared rigged or illegitimate. Over time, no external measure of merit remains credible. The only valid arbiter of the leader's greatness is the leader.

CITIZEN COUNTERMEASURES

Targeting the Wallets

Identifying the local corporate sponsors of events where the leader seeks validation allows citizens to apply direct economic pressure. By organizing negative online reviews or local boycotts of these specific sponsors' products, small groups transform the leader's presence into a financial liability. This moves the resistance from elite boardrooms to the marketplace, where ordinary consumer choices immediately increase the cost of the leader's vanity.

Ridiculing the Titles and Trophies

Transforming the leader's obsession with titles into a source of ridicule strips the honors of their protective power. Circulating memes, editorial cartoons, and satirical commentary that highlight the absurdity of the specific accolades pierces the intended aura of greatness. This recontextualization breaks the spell of authority, turning the leader's demand for respect into a public display of insecurity.

Calling Out the Ego

Depicting the leader's outrage at rejected honors as psychological fragility thwarts the mobilization of the base. Consistently highlighting the outbursts as insecurity and weakness of character focuses the lens on the individual's ego and vanity rather than national honor. This clinical detachment denies the leader the opportunity to turn their personal vanity into a national cause.

NAPOLEON'S
GRAIN
I CAN DO WHATEVER I WANT.
YOU CAN'T DO THAT!

Impunity Instinct

DEFINITION

The Impunity Instinct is the belief that laws are for other people. To the authoritarian, constitutions and treaties are fences built to pen in the weak, and the weak are, by definition, anyone who is not them. "Legality" becomes purely transactional: statutes are valid when they punish enemies, and illegitimate when they restrict the leader's own impulses. This compels the regime to ignore precedents, abuse norms, and re-interpret settled law for personal benefit. Yet these maneuvers are mere camouflage, constructed to justify a simple, absolute conviction: that the leader is entitled to do whatever they please.

EXAMPLE

A leader ascends to power and erases the line between the person and the office. The Treasury is treated as a personal bank account and the Justice Department as a private law firm. When challenged by courts or legislatures, the regime rejects the legitimacy of the check itself. State lawyers are deployed to unearth arcane statutes or invent novel legal theories, dressing up personal power grabs in the language of "executive privilege" or "national security." Subordinates are quickly purged if they prioritize the constitution over the leader's whims, replaced by loyalists who view obstruction and perjury as badges of honor. The defense is always the same: to investigate the leader is to attack the nation, because in the mind of the authoritarian, they are one and the same.

TELLTALE SIGNS OF IMPUNITY INSTINCT

The Personalization of the State

The leader erases the distinction between their private interests and the public trust. They treat the agencies of government as the departments of a corporation they own. In this worldview, civil servants, prosecutors, and generals are employees that exist solely to do the leader's bidding.

The Rejection of Oversight as "Attack"

The leader disputes the incriminating findings of investigations while attacking the legitimacy of the investigators. Any attempt to enforce accountability by the courts, legislature, press, or inspectors general, is declared a "witch hunt" or treason. The leader cannot conceive of a neutral check on their power. They view every constraint as a partisan act of war by a subordinate.

The "Law for Thee, Not for Me" Doctrine

The leader aggressively enforces the law against opponents while demanding total exemption for themselves and their allies. They use the pardon power to protect loyalists and the regulatory state to punish enemies. This is a structural belief that the law is a weapon to be wielded by the strong against the weak, never a net that catches the ruler.

IF I DO IT, IT'S LEGAL

CITIZEN COUNTERMEASURES

Shifting the Cost of Collaboration

The leader may be immune to the law, but their architects are not. This strategy targets the consultants, lawyers, donors, and technocrats who facilitate the regime. By subjecting these proxies to professional sanctions, consumer boycotts, and civil liability, citizens impose a tangible cost on collaboration. The leader can issue illegal orders, but if the machinery of execution is deterred by the certainty of professional and financial ruin, the impunity is paralyzed.

Spotting the Pattern

Authoritarians benefit from the fog of the present, where citizens often fail to recognize the danger of a current leader until it is too late. "The Historical Lens" involves relentlessly comparing current actions to the behaviors of past tyrants. By anchoring modern abuses to historical atrocities, the citizenry transfers the clarity of hindsight to the moment. This conditioned association pierces the veil of normalcy, revealing the leader's true nature by placing them in the company they deserve.

Pulling the Welcome Mat

Impunity rests on the assumption that the leader is the state. Countering this requires stripping away the ceremonial deference that masks their lawlessness. The strategy involves treating the leader as a usurper. Refusing the standard courtesies of office and turning official visits into protests, punctures the aura of invincibility. It signals that while the leader holds power, they have lost respect and authority.

BARNYARD OLYMPICS
1
2
3
THAT'S HIS FIFTH GOLD MEDAL.
IT'S WEIRD THAT EVERYONE ELSE IS TOO SICK TO RUN.

Machiavellianism

DEFINITION

Machiavellianism is a calculated approach to social and political interaction that views human beings as disposable assets to be manipulated for the acquisition of power. It is characterized by high cynicism, emotional detachment, and a utilitarian view of morality where the ends always justify the means. Unlike impulsive or emotional manipulation, this is a "cold" cognitive strategy; deceptions and betrayals are planned with the same foresight used in military campaigns. The leader excels at reading the vulnerabilities of opponents and allies alike, leveraging fear, greed, and vanity to orchestrate outcomes that consolidate their control. This trait is recognized as a core component of the "Dark Tetrad" personality profile, alongside narcissism, psychopathy, and sadism.

EXAMPLE

A regime buckles under mass protests, but the leader behaves with chilling detachment. They publicly vow to defend the capital to the death while secretly back-channeling an exit deal with the opposition or foreign powers. The leader gathers incriminating evidence against their own generals and inner circle, packaging it as currency for a plea deal. In the final hours, they trade state secrets for personal immunity, offering up their most loyal enforcers as sacrificial lambs to the mob. When the palace gates are finally breached, the throne is empty. The state collapses into revolution, but the leader survives in comfortable exile, having negotiated their safety by selling out the very people they led.

TELLTALE SIGNS OF MACHIAVELLIANISM

Instrumentalization of Relationships

The leader views every interaction solely through the lens of utility. Colleagues, family members, and long-term allies are supported only as long as they provide a strategic advantage, then ruthlessly discarded or scapegoated when they become liabilities. This pattern of "use and abuse" reveals that connections are based more on calculations of current political market value than shared values or loyalty.

Intentional Ambiguity

The leader intentionally cultivates vague positions and contradictory statements to maintain tactical flexibility. By avoiding clear commitments, they retain the ability to pivot without accountability, leaving subordinates and the public unsure of the true directive. This strategic fog forces everyone to project their own hopes onto the leader while providing endless avenues for plausible deniability when plans fail.

Triangulation of Subordinates

Control is maintained by fostering structured conflict within the inner circle. The leader privately disparages one lieutenant to another, encouraging rivalry and suspicion to prevent any collective action against the top. By keeping subordinates focused on destroying each other for the leader's favor, the regime ensures that the only stable source of power and mediation remains the leader themselves.

CITIZEN COUNTERMEASURES

Mapping the Betrayals

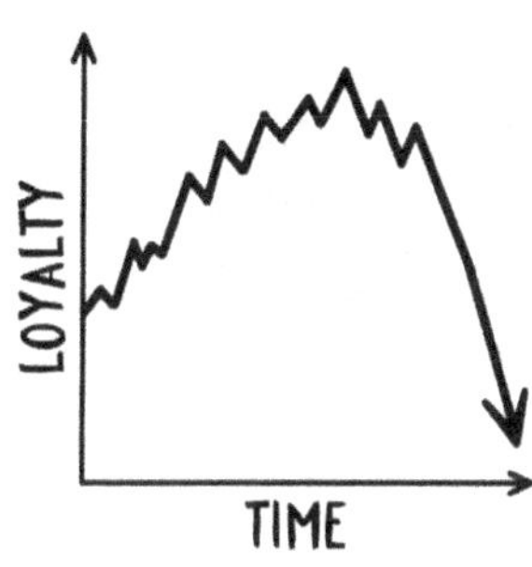

Creating a public ledger of the leader's past alliances and betrayals exposes the cyclical nature of their loyalty. By mapping the timeline of discarded allies, citizens and elites can visualize the inevitable trajectory of their own relationship with the leader. This data visualization punctures the charm, revealing that current favor is merely a temporary phase before eventual disposal.

Rejecting False Choices

Machiavellians thrive by forcing opponents into false dilemmas or "lesser of two evils" traps. Countering this requires rejecting the binary choice and introducing a third option that prioritizes institutional integrity over personality. By adhering strictly to procedural norms and refusing to engage in the leader's transactional bargaining, the opposition denies the manipulator the leverage points needed to divide and conquer.

OR

Teaching the Script

The Machiavellian makes targets feel uniquely understood and valued. Educational campaigns that decode these specific seduction techniques, such as "love bombing" and mirroring, act as a psychological firewall. When individuals recognize that the intense praise they are receiving is a standardized recruitment script rather than genuine appreciation, the emotional hook of the manipulation is severed.

MONTHLY REVIEW
OLLIE ✓
~~MEG~~
SNOWBALL
DINAH
OLLIE
MEG
YOU ARE THE GREATEST LEADER OF ALL TIME.
SNOWBALL
DINAH

Malignant Narcissism

DEFINITION

Malignant Narcissism is the toxic convergence of extreme grandiosity, paranoia, and antisocial aggression. It is an unrelenting predatory drive where the self must be exalted at all costs, and any challenge is perceived as a threat. In the mind of the authoritarian, this produces a worldview divided strictly between worshippers and enemies. The leader's identity is one with the national identity, making personal humiliation indistinguishable from national betrayal. Consequently, violence is a calculated enforcement mechanism. The leader orchestrates terror to coerce the world into validating their delusional supremacy, effectively punishing reality until it complies with their will. This trait is recognized as a core component of the "Dark Tetrad" personality profile, alongside Machiavellianism, psychopathy, and sadism.

EXAMPLE

A leader convenes a televised congress of their inner circle. As a list of "traitors" is read aloud, guards drag members from their seats one by one. The leader watches from the podium, displaying theatrical emotion while recounting the heartbreaking cruelty inflicted upon them by the disloyalty of others. The remaining audience rises to chant the leader's name, praising the leader's wisdom as colleagues are marched to their executions. This is the defining feature: the demand that the survivors not only witness the cruelty but applaud it.

TRAITORS

☒ BESSIE
☒ SNOWBALL
☒ BRUTUS
☒ HAMILTON
☒ FRITZY

TELLTALE SIGNS OF MALIGNANT NARCISSISM

Narcissistic Rage

When a malignant narcissist is criticized (or worse, humiliated), they explode. Look for a leader who cannot let a slight go. They engage in disproportionate, often self-destructive attacks against journalists, judges, or allies who fail to praise them. The leader is willing to damage their own political standing just to soothe the pain of the ego wound.

Sadistic Aggression

This pathology includes a drive to destroy and humiliate others to validate their own superiority. Watch for a leader who mocks opponents, encourages violence against them, or delights in the distress of vulnerable groups. The cruelty is a source of psychological fuel. Making others feel small makes the leader feel big.

Pathological Entitlement

To the malignant narcissist, the question is never what they have earned. It is only what they deserve, and the answer is always everything: awards, legal immunity, lifetime rule, a personal cut of every contract signed in their name. Watch for a leader who treats public funds as personal piggy banks, demands accolades or awards without merit, or claims that laws written for citizens do not apply to them.

CITIZEN COUNTERMEASURES

Applying the "Gray Rock" Protocol

The malignant narcissist subsists on attention, viewing even hatred as a form of tribute. Cutting this supply requires a disciplined collective silence known as the "Gray Rock" protocol. Instead of amplifying every outrage, the opposition reacts to policy, but ignores the person. This refusal to engage denies the leader the validation they crave.

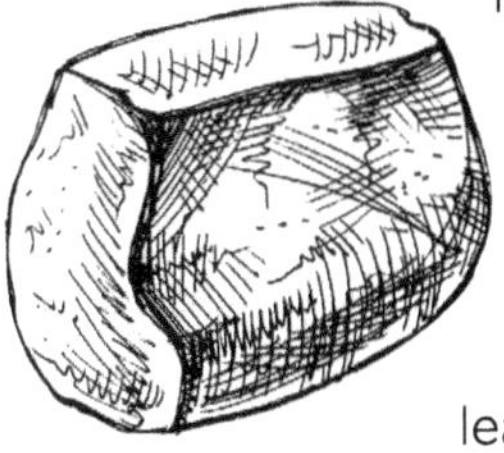

Exposing the Fragility

Utilizing satire or calculated disrespect, resistance movements can goad the leader into public meltdowns over trivial slights. When a head of state rages against a comedian or creates a crisis over a minor insult, the contrast between their office and their behavior becomes undeniable. This tactic transforms the leader's aggression into evidence of instability, shattering the image of the stoic strongman.

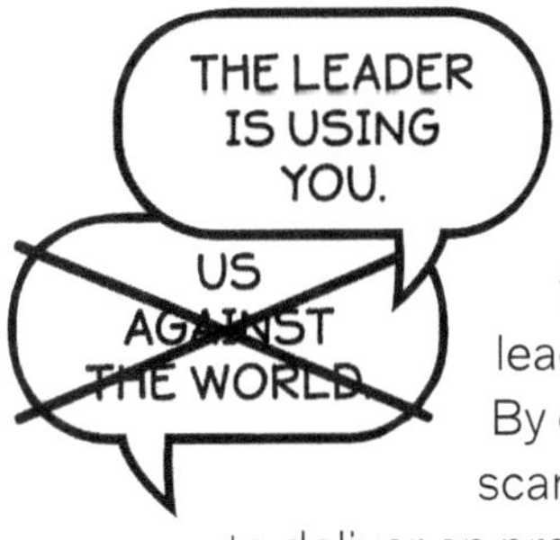

Revealing Contempt for the Base

The bond between the narcissist and their base is built on a shared fantasy of mutual persecution. Severing this connection requires revealing the leader's contempt for their own believers. By documenting the private insults, the scams targeting supporters, and the failure to deliver on promises, the narrative shifts from "Us against the World" to "The Leader Is Using You." Once the follower realizes they are merely a prop in the leader's manipulation, their loyalty curdles into betrayal.

CHOSEN TO SAVE THE FARM

Messianic Complex

DEFINITION

The Messianic Complex is the authoritarian delusion of destiny. It casts the leader as a figure chosen by god or fate to save a fallen nation. This complex blends extreme narcissism with authoritarian control, frequently appearing in leaders who perceive themselves as infallible and destined for greatness. The disorder often begins as performative piety, a cynical pantomime of faith designed to court the devout. Yet, over time, the performance seduces the performer. The tyrant consumes their own propaganda, interpreting the survival of scandals and crises as proof of their providence. They become convinced that they are exempt from ordinary law because their mission is ordained by a higher power. Politics is transfigured into a sacred mission where compromise is heresy and opposition is evil.

EXAMPLE

A leader rises from the ashes of crisis, wrapping themselves in the symbols of the dominant faith while violating its tenets in private. They pose as the defender of a besieged tradition, using religion as a lever to pry open the halls of power. But as the rallies grow and the enemies fall, the cynicism hardens into conviction. The narrative becomes absolute: the nation was lost, and only this leader was fated to find it. Laws are ignored because the mission is said to transcend human law. Atrocities are justified as holy work. Loyalty evolves into faith, dissent morphs into blasphemy, and the leader comes to believe they are the state's divinely sanctioned redeemer.

TELLTALE SIGNS OF MESSIANIC COMPLEX

The Doctrine of Destiny

The leader views their authority as a divine mandate. They cast themselves as a "chosen one" or prophet, claiming unique powers to solve complex problems that paralyze ordinary institutions. By presenting themselves as the sole source of help and the only barrier against impending catastrophe, they transform governance into a theology where they alone can rescue the nation.

Apocalyptic Polarization

To the Messianic leader, political opposition is heresy. Such leaders divide the world into absolute binary terms of light and darkness. Critics are portrayed as "demons," "vermin," or fundamental threats to the soul of the nation. This rhetoric transforms governance into a holy war, justifying any atrocity as a necessary act of purification.

The Demand for Tribute

The leader displays an exaggerated sense of self-importance, viewing the state as a vessel for their own validation. They operate with a pathological entitlement, craving constant adoration and praise to sustain their grandiose self-image. This insatiable need for tribute transforms the political sphere into an echo chamber, where the loyalty of the follower is measured by the volume of their worship.

CITIZEN COUNTERMEASURES

Popping the Bubble

Messianic leaders rely on awe to sustain their authority; they require the public to look up. Countering this requires stripping away the sacred aura through relentless satire. By highlighting physical vanities, absurdities, and pettiness, the opposition reduces a deity to a caricature. A "savior" can survive hatred, which validates their importance, but they cannot survive laughter, which exposes their smallness.

Doing a Reality Check

The leader trades in prophecies and abstract enemies to distract from reality. Countering this involves aggressively grounding political discourse in the mundane. By measuring the "chosen one" against the concrete metrics of governance—potholes, prices, and public services—citizens force a contrast between the promise of salvation and the reality of decline. This reveals the leader as an incompetent manager rather than a divine protector.

Exposing the Scam

The bond between the leader and the base is forged in shared victimhood. Severing this requires revealing the relationship to be exploitative—which it invariably is. By documenting how the leader enriches themselves at the followers' expense through scams, neglect, or private disdain, the narrative shifts. The follower realizes they are no longer a disciple in a holy war, but the mark in a long con.

PINCHFIELD FARM
CERTIFIED AUTOCRAT
THE MANOR FARM
STOP STEALING OUR EGGS
I CAN MAKE YOUR PROBLEM GO AWAY.
THE FAVOR WILL BE RETURNED.
TYRANT

Predatory Kinship

DEFINITION

Predatory Kinship is an instinctive affinity for fellow tyrants, driven by a mix of psychological comfort and transactional utility. The authoritarian instinctively divides leaders into "sheepdogs"—anxious guardians hemmed in by oversight—and "wolves"—creatures of pure will who recognize no boundary but superior force. This species division creates a strategic preference for the "wolf." Autocrats recognize one another as reliable partners because they can buy and trade favors in ways that are impossible with a rule-of-law state. Tools of influence that fail against checks and balances like bribery and blackmail work perfectly between dictators. The bond is forged in the conviction that while democracies argue, tyrants deal and get things done.

EXAMPLE

An authoritarian faces international sanctions or domestic legal threats. Instead of conforming to the law, they pivot to a friendly strongman for a lifeline. A partner provides untraceable loans and diplomatic cover at the United Nations. In return, favors flow back: votes are blocked, dissidents are extradited, and state resources are swapped like poker chips. The relationship deepens through these repeated quid pro quos, strengthening a partnership serving private interests rather than national strategy. Governance devolves into an informal cartel, operating to ensure that the leaders live large and remain in power.

TELLTALE SIGNS OF PREDATORY KINSHIP

Celebrating Autocratic Efficiency

The leader frequently praises the "strength" and "decisiveness" of foreign dictators, contrasting their unchecked power with the perceived weakness of democratic deliberation. By equating repression with efficiency and due process with obstruction, the regime signals a desire to emulate authoritarian methods. This rhetoric normalizes the "strongman" model as superior to the rule of law.

Privatization of Diplomatic Channels

The regime bypasses established diplomatic channels in favor of off-the-record, personal interactions with fellow autocrats. Because rule-of-law states cannot offer personal favors or immunity, the leader pivots toward counterparts who can engage in bribery, secret pacts, or mutual protection without institutional oversight. This shifts foreign policy from a pursuit of national interest to a mechanism for personal enrichment and regime security.

Reciprocal Defense of Impunity

The leader consistently defends foreign atrocities as internal matters of sovereignty, shielding fellow autocrats from international sanctions or human rights criticism. By eroding global norms against repression, the regime preemptively establishes a defense for its own future abuses. This alignment creates a de facto alliance of impunity, where dictators provide reciprocal cover to block external pressure and legitimate domestic crackdowns.

CITIZEN COUNTERMEASURES

Highlighting the Subservience
Predatory kinship relies on the projection of shared strength. By documenting how the leader makes unfavorable concessions to please the foreign autocrat, the narrative shifts from "two wolves" to a relationship of subservience. This punctures the "strongman" image by revealing the leader's desperation for foreign approval.

Protecting Neighbors
Authoritarian alliances often involve "transnational repression," where the foreign dictator harasses dissidents living within the domestic leader's borders. Establishing community watch networks and legal defense funds for these diaspora groups disrupts this collusion. Providing physical presence and visibility for threatened exiles prevents the domestic regime from quietly facilitating the foreign partner's vengeance.

Cutting the Cash Flow
While citizens cannot dictate federal sanctions, they hold leverage over local capital. Petitioning municipal governments, university endowments, and public pension funds to divest from the partner regime creates a distributed economic blockade. Moving these specific, manageable pools of capital creates a "bottom-up" financial penalty that bypasses federal inaction and imposes a tangible cost on the foreign autocrat's economy.

YOU KNOW IT'S FRIED EGG FRIDAY.
WHAT HAPPENED?

Psychopathy

DEFINITION

Psychopathy is a severe personality disorder characterized by antisocial behavior, irresponsibility, criminality, and a failure to learn from punishment. While many individuals possess isolated psychopathic traits, the clinical psychopath represents the most extreme manifestation of the disorder, usually a product of a distinct neurological predisposition compounded by early environmental trauma. In the mind of an authoritarian, this manifests as a total moral vacuum. Citizens are reduced to inputs, obstacles, or expendable resources. Violence is not considered a method of last resort, but rather a neutral instrument, deployed without hesitation if it serves power. There is no inner brake. No guilt to overcome. No consideration for human cost. This trait is recognized as a core component of the "Dark Tetrad" personality profile, alongside narcissism, Machiavellianism, and sadism.

EXAMPLE

A leader targets a vulnerable sub-population, such as immigrants or a religious minority, identifying them as a contaminant in the national body. To operationalize this impulse, they rely on a cadre of loyal enablers who translate their malice into administrative procedures. Legal advisors draft the rationale to circumvent human rights, while spokespeople spin the brutality as national security. Human beings are categorized, numbered, and herded into camps like livestock. When confronted with the visceral reality of the suffering, including crying children, separated parents, and squalid conditions, the leader displays a terrifying indifference. The brutality is public, yet the leader sleeps soundly, insulated by a complete inability to feel the pain of another.

TELLTALE SIGNS OF PSYCHOPATHY

The Disposal of "Used" Allies

For the psychopath, loyalty is a one-way street. They view human beings strictly as tools to be used and discarded. The telltale sign is a history of discarding longtime loyalists, mentors, or "friends" the moment they become a liability or cease to be useful. There is no sentimental attachment, no hesitation, and no "thank you for your service." The ally is simply erased.

The Cold Calculation of Revenge

Watch how the leader handles public criticism. The psychopath reacts with cold strategy. They do not lose control. They take inventory. If crossed, they may smile or remain eerily calm in the moment. But six months later, the critic is arrested, bankrupted, or purged. The tell is the unnatural silence followed by a precise, disproportionate destruction of the enemy.

A "Flat" Reaction to Tragedy

The psychopath often fails to mimic the correct emotion when confronted with suffering. Look for a leader who seems bored, indifferent, or even subtly amused ("duping delight") during moments of national tragedy or when discussing victims of their policies. They may read a prepared statement of condolence, but their eyes remain dead and their tone robotic. The biological hardware for shared pain is missing.

CITIZEN COUNTERMEASURES

Focusing on the Enablers

A psychopathic leader cannot implement mass cruelty alone; they require a circle of bureaucrats, lawyers, and officers who may not be psychopaths themselves but are "following orders" out of ambition or fear. These individuals do have a breaking point. Effective resistance efforts focus on these enablers, naming them, shaming them, and raising the social and legal costs of their collaboration. When the enablers defect, the regime loses its hands.

Abandoning Appeals to Conscience

The most common mistake citizens make is projecting their own morality onto the leader. They write open letters, stage emotional protests, or plead for mercy, believing that if the leader just understood the suffering, they would stop. This is a waste of time. The psychopath does not have the biological hardware to process shame or empathy. Your tears are not a deterrent. They are a source of validation. Stop trying to persuade the leader. Direct all communication and appeals to the public, the courts, and the international community.

Raising the Price of Cruelty

Psychopaths are transactional. They are not motivated by ideology or the "greater good," but by self-interest and survival. To change their behavior, you must stop arguing about what is right and make oppression expensive. Protests, strikes, and sanctions must threaten their power base or personal wealth. Appeals to the heart are ineffective; instead, the focus shifts to their wallet and their need for control. If the cost of the cruelty outweighs the benefit, they will drop it.

BENEFIT

COST

CRUELTY

THEY ALWAYS CRY AT FIRST.

Sadism

DEFINITION

Sadism is a pathological orientation toward power in which the infliction of suffering becomes emotionally rewarding. Unlike cruelty that is instrumental or ideologically justified, sadism involves a direct psychological payoff from another's pain, fear, or humiliation. The sadistic leader finds in suffering proof of their power. Pain is used to regulate the leader's emotional state, replacing insecurity with a sense of omnipotence. Over time, cruelty ceases to serve governance at all. It becomes self-reinforcing. Authority is no longer validated through order or loyalty, but through the visible breaking of others. This trait is recognized as a core component of the "Dark Tetrad" personality profile, alongside narcissism, Machiavellianism, and psychopathy.

EXAMPLE

A regime transforms the state's security headquarters into a theater of suffering. The leader is known to personally visit the "interrogation" rooms to watch rivals be tortured. In a display of ultimate dominance, the bodies of high-ranking judges, archbishops, or cabinet members are abandoned in public spaces or even displayed in morgues for families to find. This violence is not a tool for gathering intelligence—most victims are dead or broken before they can speak—but rather a ritual of "expressive" power. By treating human life as disposable and the human body as a canvas for humiliation, the leader transforms cruelty into a governing norm. Subordinates come to fear the appetite behind the orders as much as the orders themselves.

TELLTALE SIGNS OF SADISM

Seeking Satisfaction in Suffering

The primary indicator is a direct psychological payoff derived from witnessing or inflicting harm on any living being. This includes a documented history of animal abuse, coupled with evident pleasure in witnessing beings suffer. Unlike violence used to achieve a goal, this cruelty is pursued for the emotional reward of the spectacle.

Personalizing the Infliction of Pain

A sadistic individual tends to be intimately involved in the suffering they cause. They may refuse to delegate punishment, preferring to watch, taunt, or participate directly in the victim's agony. This "personal touch" confirms that the violence is a deeply felt preference for exercising absolute, unchecked control over another's physical or emotional state.

Using Arbitrary and Escalating Cruelty

Sadism often manifests as a pattern of unpredictable punishment where the rules are constantly shifting. This ensures that the target remains in a state of perpetual terror, never knowing what might trigger an attack. As the "payoff" from standard cruelty diminishes, the sadist frequently escalates the intensity or intimacy of the violence to maintain the same level of satisfaction.

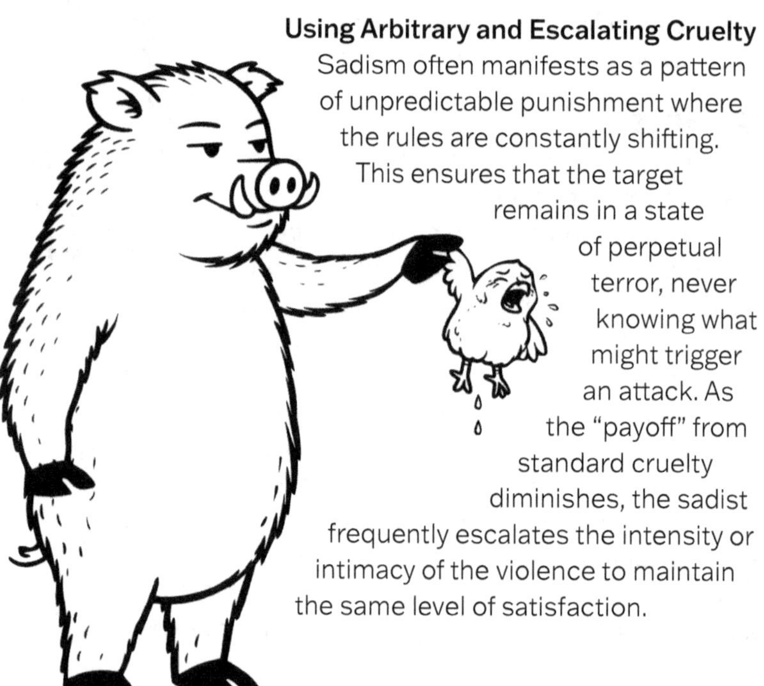

CITIZEN COUNTERMEASURES

Isolating the Audience

Sadism thrives on theatrical power, for cruelty unwitnessed is cruelty unfelt. By coordinating a collective refusal to attend "shame rituals" or participate in public mockery, the group denies the leader the psychological payoff they crave. When the community maintains a stoic, silent presence, the show of cruelty fails to gain social momentum, leaving the sadist psychologically isolated and their power looking hollow.

Creating Anonymized Reporting Channels

Because a sadist targets individuals for personal degradation, survivors must establish secret, encrypted

ways to document abuses without immediate

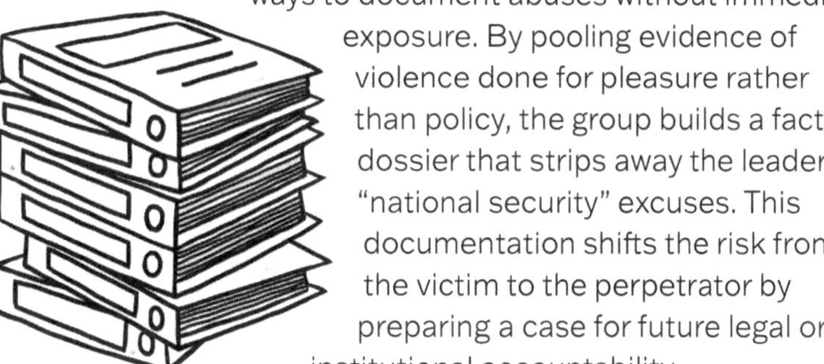

exposure. By pooling evidence of violence done for pleasure rather than policy, the group builds a factual dossier that strips away the leader's "national security" excuses. This documentation shifts the risk from the victim to the perpetrator by preparing a case for future legal or institutional accountability.

Reclaiming Victim Identity

A sadistic leader attempts to destroy a victim's spirit by branding them as a "traitor" or "failure" before hurting them. Counteracting this requires the community to actively "humanize" those targeted, refusing to use the leader's derogatory language. By celebrating the victim's true character and providing secret support to their family, the group proves that the leader can break the body but cannot rewrite the victim's story or the community's values.

STAGE II

The Fabrication of Reality

A tyrant without followers is merely a madman. To feed, the *Tyrannus Rex* must export its delusion to the masses. This stage charts the transition from individual pathology to collective psychosis. Driven by natural predilections, the creature becomes an astute student of control, often sharpening these dark arts in the service of an existing power. This is the proving ground where the predator earns its credibility. Acting as an influential operative circling the throne, it reverse-engineers the tactics of past regimes to dismantle the concept of objective truth, waiting for the precise moment to elevate its standing and seize the mantle. With the information landscape poisoned and the past rewritten, the aspirant constructs a controlled ecosystem where reality is fluid. To resist, we must become the stubborn witnesses of truth. Drawing from the playbooks of censorship and control, we isolate ten mechanisms of distortion to clear the fog. We map the narrative. We expose the edits. We shatter the illusion to reclaim the record.

IN THIS STAGE

Accusation in a Mirror • Astroturfing • Big Lie • DARVO
Firehose of Falsehood • Gaslighting • Media Capture
Newspeak • Rewriting History • War on Expertise

FEED ROOM
THE DONKEYS ARE STEALING FOOD!
GRAIN

Accusation in a Mirror

DEFINITION

Accusation in a Mirror (AiM) is a propaganda tactic in which an authoritarian accuses opponents of the very wrongdoing they are committing. By projecting their own nefarious intentions onto others, the regime preempts accusations or discovery of its own malfeasance. The tactic works because it neutralizes criticism before it lands: if both sides are accused of the same offense, many citizens disengage, unsure whom to believe. This ambiguity creates political cover for the authoritarian's actual abuses, allowing them to continue unchecked. Originating in genocidal rhetoric and now common in modern disinformation systems, accusation in a mirror transforms projection into a weapon and immunizes the regime against accountability.

EXAMPLE

A ruling faction preparing for mass violence begins by warning that its targeted minority is plotting exactly the kind of attack the faction itself intends to carry out. Party officials and aligned media outlets repeat claims that the minority group is arming for genocide, infiltrating institutions, or conspiring to eliminate the majority. These warnings escalate in urgency and detail even though no credible evidence is ever produced. State-aligned broadcasters describe imaginary atrocities and attribute them to the very people the regime plans to persecute. When violence eventually erupts, many interpret it as preemptive defense. The inversion reshapes public perception so completely that the perpetrators appear as protectors and the victims as existential threats.

TELLTALE SIGNS OF ACCUSATION IN A MIRROR

Reflecting Known Intentions

The most telling sign is the uncanny, specific nature of the accusation itself. For instance, a regime that is actively plotting to rig an election will consistently accuse its opponents of "plotting to steal the election." The accusation directly mirrors the perpetrator's own hidden agenda, effectively turning their future crime into a preemptive political defense.

Everything is an Existential Threat

The opponent is presented as a life-or-death threat. The leader consistently warns that the opponent is planning to "destroy," "wipe out," "subvert," or "enslave" their constituency. This extreme language is crucial because it leverages the psychological mechanism of collective self-defense, making the audience believe the leader's subsequent destructive actions are necessary and justified.

A Lack of Supporting Evidence

Despite the gravity of the accusation, there is an absence of credible evidence for the mirrored claim (e.g., no proof of the victim group plotting an uprising). Conversely, the targeted group will issue strong, unambiguous denials of the mirrored accusation. This tactic relies on making the public believe that because two sides are locked in a rhetorical struggle, the truth must lie in the middle.

CITIZEN COUNTERMEASURES

Demanding the Proof

WHERE IS THE PROOF?

The refusal to accept accusations as a pretext for immediate action interrupts the mobilization cycle. Publicly demanding verifiable evidence to support claims of imminent threats serves to expose the lack of justification. This disrupts the psychological mechanism that positions the leader's planned aggression as necessary self-defense.

Supporting the Accused

Breaking the regime's monopoly on the narrative involves the amplification of denials of the targeted group. Validating these statements through independent channels highlights the evidentiary imbalance. This contrast clarifies that the threatened action is a political maneuver rather than a response to a genuine security threat.

Exposing the Pretext

Analyzing AiM claims as deliberate pretexts reveals the underlying agenda. Once citizens recognize that every accusation is a confession, the rhetorical inversion collapses into a self-incriminating prophecy. Linking the specific accusation to the regime's known goals exposes the fabrication, redefining the narrative from one of defensive necessity to one of calculated aggression.

EAT
MORE
GOATS
WE GET EXTRA FOOD FOR JUST STANDING HERE.
VOTE

Astroturfing

DEFINITION

Astroturfing is the deliberate fabrication of "grassroots" support to create the illusion of popular demand where none exists. Instead of persuading citizens, the regime simulates them. Paid operatives, bot networks, front groups, and coordinated influencers flood media, rallies, comment sections, and hashtags with pre-scripted messages presented as spontaneous public opinion. The tactic exploits a basic social proof heuristic: people assume that widely shared views must be legitimate. By faking consensus, astroturfing pressures fence-sitters to conform and supplies elites with a false mandate. It also muddies attribution, making authentic civic action harder to distinguish from manipulation. Over time, citizens stop trusting crowds altogether, and the loudest signal wins by default.

EXAMPLE

A divisive election approaches. A social media campaign appears to "break through," claiming to represent a surge of ordinary citizens abandoning one party or cause. The messaging spreads at unnatural speed, propelled by clusters of newly created or recycled accounts repeating identical slogans and hashtags. Foreign-linked bot networks amplify the campaign, launder its talking points through sympathetic influencers, and target specific voter blocs with tailored content designed to suppress turnout. Traditional media cite the trend as evidence of a groundswell. Officials point to it as proof of public will. What looks like a grassroots movement is actually a coordinated information operation designed to persuade targeted citizens not to vote.

TELLTALE SIGNS OF ASTROTURFING

The Cut-and-Paste Effect

Genuine grassroots movements are messy. Individuals express shared grievances in unique ways. Astroturfing relies on centralized scripts, resulting in unnatural uniformity. This manifests as identical phrases, slogans, or specific keywords appearing simultaneously across thousands of unconnected accounts or protest signs. When "independent" voices recite the exact same talking points, it signals a distributed script rather than organic consensus.

The Instant Spike

Real movements typically build momentum over time as awareness spreads. Astroturfing campaigns exhibit massive spikes in activity that appear instantly, often coinciding perfectly with a political objective. If a hashtag trends globally minutes after its first use, or thousands of accounts activate simultaneously at 9:00 AM to comment on a policy, the coordination is likely logistical, not social.

The Sockpuppet Profile

Astroturfing relies on volume, often necessitating fake accounts ("sockpuppets"). These profiles betray themselves through a lack of history: they often have recent creation dates, generic or stolen profile photos, and timelines devoid of personal content. If a user's history consists exclusively of retweeting a single narrative without any other human interaction, it is likely a deployed asset rather than a citizen.

CITIZEN COUNTERMEASURES

Revealing the Coordination

Treating a sudden wave of support as a dataset rather than a debate facilitates the identification of artificial patterns. By documenting identical timestamps, verbatim phrasing across unconnected accounts, and synchronized creation dates, activists can reveal the centralized structure of the campaign. Publishing this forensic evidence dismantles the illusion of consensus, proving that thousands of distinct "voices" are merely echoing a single source.

Predicting the Script

Publicly predicting the arrival of artificial support diminishes its psychological impact. When communities are warned that a specific fabricated narrative is about to be deployed (e.g., "expect bot networks to flood the zone with [Specific Claim] tomorrow"), they process the subsequent influx as manipulation rather than social proof. This transforms the astroturfing attempt from a persuasive tactic into evidence of the regime's dishonesty.

Burning the Sockpuppets

Systematically analyzing the history of participating accounts exposes the lack of organic behavior. Credibility is verified by checking for "sockpuppet" indicators: recent creation dates, stolen profile photos, and timelines devoid of personal content. Publicizing these findings raises the operational cost for the regime, as their digital assets are identified and "burned" faster than they can be effectively replaced.

THE ELECTION
WAS RIGGED.
I WON.
THE
ELECTI
WAS
THE
ELECTIO
WAS
RIGGED
RIGGED!

Big Lie

DEFINITION

A Big Lie does not distort reality. It displaces it. The tactic exploits a paradox of human psychology in which people are more likely to doubt small lies than large ones. The technique was described by Adolf Hitler in *Mein Kampf*, and later perfected by propagandists like Joseph Goebbels. In modern form, the big lie leverages cognitive dissonance. It forces a painful collision between observable reality and the leader's rhetoric, leaving the subject with a stark choice: believe the lie or believe the leader is a liar. Followers resolve this tension by dismissing their senses and accepting the falsehood on faith, maintaining their devotion and binding them ever closer to the regime through shared delusion.

EXAMPLE

An authoritarian desires to remain in office despite losing an election. They advance a narrative that the vote was stolen through massive fraud. No credible evidence supports the claim, so they rely on endless repetition. Minor procedural errors are inflated into deep state plots. Officials who contradict the narrative are labeled traitors. The lie becomes ever bigger as time passes as the regime responds to contrary evidence by enlarging the conspiracy. The big lie isn't designed to be credible, but comforting. Faced with the cognitive dissonance that their champion lost, supporters are handed a way out: the leader is not defeated, the system is just corrupt. Given this emotionally preferable explanation, loyalists embrace the big lie and keep their faith in the leader intact.

TELLTALE SIGNS OF BIG LIE

Endless Repetition

This is the engine of the big lie. The sheer volume and consistency of repetition across speeches, state media, and pervasive slogans transforms initial skepticism into uncomfortable familiarity, and uncomfortable familiarity into uncritical conviction.

Immunity to Correction

Every counter-argument, piece of evidence, or official contradiction is advanced by the purveyors as undeniable "proof" of a wider, deeper conspiracy designed to conceal the "real truth." This self-healing, paranoia-generating quality distinguishes a true big lie from ordinary misinformation.

Scale Over Plausibility

The big lie must be too big to question and too monstrous to admit as fiction. Its function extends beyond persuasion to corrode the collective capacity for objective truth. When no external source can be trusted, the leader becomes the only stable arbiter of reality.

CITIZEN COUNTERMEASURES

Making Truth Sandwiches

Repetition reinforces belief through the "illusory truth effect." This is countered through the "truth sandwich" technique: leading and ending with verified facts while enclosing the falsehood in between. This structure ensures the truth serves as the primary cognitive anchor, preventing the lie from gaining strength through continued repetition.

Staying Stubbornly Skeptical

The big lie thrives on the demand for absolute certainty. Promoting a culture of skepticism where "extraordinary claims require extraordinary evidence" creates a cognitive barrier against this manipulation. The questioning of narratives that allege vast conspiracies or demand unquestioning loyalty serves to introduce necessary friction. This disciplined inquiry slows the emotional speed required for mass deception to take root.

Telling an Evidence-Based Story

Big lies endure because they offer simple, emotionally satisfying stories for complex events. Effective debunking requires filling the resulting causal gap with a clear, evidence-based alternative. Replacing the fiction with a compelling factual narrative satisfies the psychological need for coherence, preventing the audience from reverting to the fabricated explanation.

STOP! YOU'RE HURTING HIM.
NO I'M NOT. YOU'RE A LIAR. QUIT ATTACKING ME.

DARVO

DEFINITION

DARVO—an acronym for Deny, Attack, and Reverse Victim and Offender—is a manipulative strategy used by abusers, institutions, and authoritarians alike to evade accountability. The sequence is simple but effective: first deny the wrongdoing, then attack the accuser's credibility, and finally reverse the roles of victim and offender so that the perpetrator appears persecuted and the accuser appears malicious. Originally identified in the study of interpersonal abuse, DARVO has since become a common tactic in political communication and propaganda. By swiftly counter-claiming victimhood, the aggressor muddies the waters, transforming a clear violation into a symmetrical "conflict." This paralyzes public judgment and forces the accuser to defend their own character rather than the crime.

EXAMPLE

An authoritarian regime is accused of election fraud. Rather than addressing the charge, the leader denies it outright, calling it "fabricated" or "politically motivated." Next, the regime attacks the accusers, publicly berating them as "stupid" and "incompetent," and often branding them as "foreign agents" or "traitors." The focus shifts from the wrongdoing to the supposed malevolence of those exposing it. Finally, the leader reverses the roles of victim and offender. They claim that *they* are the true target of persecution. The narrative becomes "we are under attack." Supporters, emotionally engaged by the injustice, rally to the leader's defense. The original wrongdoing fades from view, replaced by a drama of grievance and retribution.

TELLTALE SIGNS OF DARVO

Step 1: Denial

The perpetrator's first move is aggressive denial, delivered with faux outrage or confusion regardless of the evidence. This immediately resets the exchange: the accuser, who moments ago held the moral high ground, must now defend the basic facts of their own account. The perpetrator has not answered the accusation. They have replaced it with a new question: can the accuser be believed at all?

Step 2: Attack

Instead of addressing the accusation, the manipulator attacks the accuser's credibility. They introduce irrelevant past errors, charge the accuser with dishonesty, or suggest they are "crazy" or "lying for attention." This tactic aims to make the accuser's character the central problem, not the original offense.

Step 3: Reverse Victim and Offender

The final step is the strategic shift of roles. The manipulator claims that they are the true victim of the accuser's "attack," "false accusation," or "betrayal." They demand sympathy, leveraging their own distress to make the accuser feel guilty for having raised the initial complaint, thereby evading responsibility entirely.

CITIZEN COUNTERMEASURES

Repeating the Facts

The strategy of ignoring personal attacks and refusing to debate emotional rhetoric denies the aggressor the conflict they seek. The "broken record" technique anchors the interaction in reality: ignore the attacks, pivot back, and repeat the verifiable facts. Every repeated fact is a brick. Lay enough of them and the manipulator has nowhere left to stand.

Highlighting the Pivot

In public settings, identifying the attack as an evasion tactic exposes the maneuver, and repeating the original inquiry forces the refusal to answer into the spotlight. If the question still goes unanswered, repetition of the inquiry by the next questioner maintains the pressure. When questioners collaborate to maintain this focus, the unified pressure defeats the attempt to silence scrutiny, transforming the attack into a visible admission of avoidance.

Laughing at the Act

Exposing aggressive attacks as a "tell" for hidden guilt inverts the tactic's power. Using satire to establish this predictable expectation teaches the public to interpret the outburst as a confessional reflex. When citizens view the behavior as farce rather than force, its capacity to intimidate collapses.

BUT BOSS, EVERYONE KNOWS THESE DOCUMENTS ARE FAKE. DOESN'T THAT PROVE THAT THE SCANDAL IS REAL?
WHO CAN TELL WHAT'S REAL ANYMORE?

Firehose of Falsehood

DEFINITION

A Firehose of Falsehood is the rapid, continuous, and high-volume delivery of information designed to overwhelm the public's ability to identify what matters or what is real. The content is irrelevant. True, false, distorted, or nonsensical, it all serves the same purpose: disorientation. By pumping out content faster than it can be checked, authoritarians exploit the overload. When people cannot verify anything, they begin to doubt everything. In this environment, factual accuracy becomes irrelevant. What counts is repetition, emotional punch, and sheer volume. Research on modern propaganda notes that the firehose model abandons traditional persuasion entirely; instead of offering one coherent lie, it sprays many incompatible stories at once, making truth impossible to locate and power the only remaining anchor.

EXAMPLE

An authoritarian faces a scandal involving evidence too massive to conceal or redact. Knowing the truth will eventually come out, the leader derides the charges as a "witch hunt," claiming that all the evidence is fake. To bolster this claim, the regime itself floods the zone with conspicuously doctored images, videos, and forged documents mixed in with the genuine evidence. When independent reviewers inevitably identify these crude forgeries, the regime seizes the moment as proof of a witch hunt. By salting the evidence with their own fakes, they successfully cast doubt on the genuine files. The legal process is paralyzed, trapped in a debate about verification rather than guilt, while supporters dismiss the entire case as a fabrication.

TELLTALE SIGNS OF FIREHOSE OF FALSEHOOD

A Barrage of Contradictory Narratives

A truthful source offers one consistent account. An authoritarian flood offers many, often contradictory, ones. The goal is not to tell a coherent lie, but to surround an inconvenient fact with a fog of confusion.

High Volume, High Speed, Low Quality

Information is produced and disseminated faster than it can be verified. Press releases, hashtags, doctored clips, "expert" blogs, and viral posts all appear in rapid succession. Each claim is disposable, but together they overload the system. By the time one falsehood is debunked, ten more have taken its place. Journalists and fact-checkers can't keep up.

Coordinated Attacks on All "Referees"

Flooding begins where truth resists. To drown it out, the regime must destroy trust in journalists, judges, scientists, and any other experts who defend it. These figures are smeared as traitors, puppets, or foreign agents, ensuring that no source remains credible. The aim is to make every truth-teller appear partisan.

CITIZEN COUNTERMEASURES

Exposing the Tactic

The firehose relies on volume to overwhelm, but its weakness is visibility. Research indicates that debunking every

falsehood is ineffective. Instead, revealing the pattern itself, showing that contradictory explanations are being released simultaneously, transforms audience perception. Shifting focus from content to method allows citizens to observe the chaos rather than drown in it, restoring necessary psychological distance.

Sticking to One Message

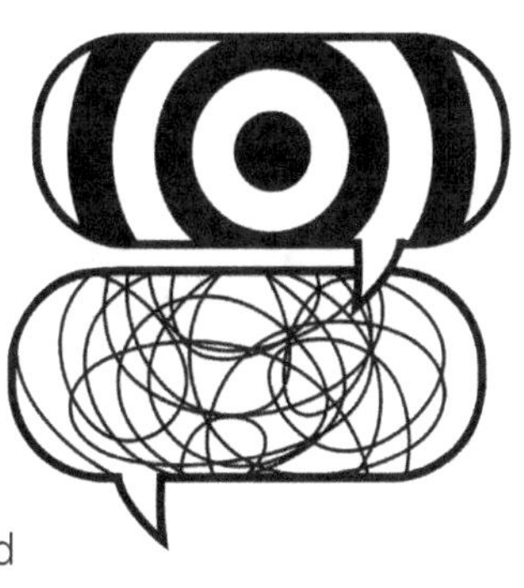

The purpose of a flood is to force truth-tellers onto the defensive. Pressure is maintained by ignoring the majority of false claims and relentlessly focusing on a single, evidence-based message. Holding one line of truth more firmly than the regime repeats its lies allows communicators to reclaim the narrative. This discipline denies the flood the confusion it requires to succeed.

Activating Trusted Local Messengers

When a flood erodes trust in major institutions, credibility must flow through smaller channels. Equipping respected local figures like doctors, teachers, or community leaders with verifiable facts creates "truth firebreaks." These local networks possess a reputational durability that national propaganda cannot easily bypass, effectively grounding the community in a shared reality despite the noise.

THE TROUGH IS FULL. YOU'VE NEVER EATEN BETTER!
BUT IT'S ALWAYS EMPTY!

Gaslighting

DEFINITION

Gaslighting is a deliberate attempt to make people doubt their own perception, memory, or judgment until they accept the manipulator's version of reality as the only truth. The tactic derives its name from the 1944 film *Gaslight*, in which a husband dims the lamps in his home and denies doing so, leading his wife to question her sanity. In authoritarian politics, gaslighting functions as a slow, psychological coup: rather than silencing dissent by force, it dissolves the very possibility of shared truth. By denying obvious facts, contradicting prior statements, and accusing others of confusion or bias, the manipulator replaces reality with an atmosphere of uncertainty in which power alone defines what is real.

EXAMPLE

An authoritarian incites a violent assault on the nation's seat of power, then immediately begins rewriting the story. At first, the attackers are hailed as patriots defending freedom. When condemnation mounts, the narrative shifts, claiming the violence was exaggerated, staged by enemies, or provoked by the opposition. Loyal media echo each revision, eroding clarity through repetition. To solidify the rewritten narrative, the authoritarian pardons the attackers, transforming them from criminals into martyrs. Eyewitnesses are dismissed as biased, recordings as fabrications, and the truth itself becomes partisan. The goal is to make citizens doubt their own senses and accept confusion as reality. In the end, the authoritarian achieves what force alone cannot: a population too disoriented to recognize what truly happened.

TELLTALE SIGNS OF GASLIGHTING

Contradictory Denial

Clear statements, events, or evidence are later flatly denied, inverted, or dismissed as "crazy," forcing the target to question their own perception rather than the gaslighter's honesty. This steady, bewildering contradiction corrodes the victim's confidence in their memory and their ability to accurately judge reality.

Projection and Blame-Shifting

The gaslighter strategically accuses others of the very deception they themselves are actively committing. This tactic successfully redirects scrutiny and reinforces the manipulator's false claim to moral authority, making them appear as the victim or the only sane person.

Erosion of Confidence

Through repeated cycles of contradictions and emotional manipulation, the target becomes fundamentally dependent on the gaslighter for cues about what is real and true. Over time, personal discernment is replaced by chronic doubt, leading to a state of dependency on the gaslighter to define reality and determine what is fact versus fiction.

CITIZEN COUNTERMEASURES

Writing it Down

Gaslighting relies on the erosion of memory to instill doubt. The maintenance of an immediate, timestamped record of contradictory statements and blatant lies is a foundational defense. Cross-referencing these records with trusted peers and independent news sources externalizes proof. This tangible evidence prevents the manipulator from rewriting history and anchors the target's perception in verifiable reality.

Establishing Boundaries

The gaslighter seeks to impose a distorted reality by engaging the target in endless debate. Disrupting this cycle requires firm cognitive boundaries: engage with facts, never with the premises of lies. Declining to participate in the contradiction protects the target's mental autonomy. This refusal to negotiate reality forces the gaslighter to expend energy without gaining psychological ground.

Comparing Notes

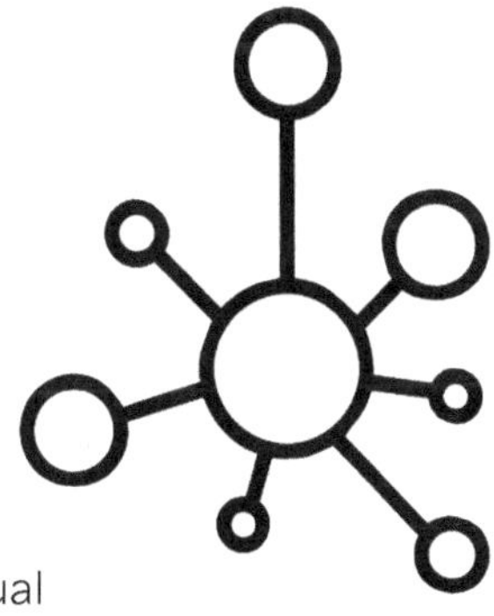

Isolation is a prerequisite for successful gaslighting. Maintaining and actively consulting a network of trusted friends who share a consistent understanding of facts is the most effective countermeasure. Regularly confirming perceptions with this group creates a "reality check" that an individual cannot achieve alone. This collective validation acts as a social shield, preventing the manipulation from taking hold.

STATE OF THE FARM
CONFERENCE
Q&A
HOW DO YOU STRUCTURE YOUR DAY?
WHAT KEEPS YOU FOCUSED?
HOW DO YOU STAY SO DISCIPLINED?

Media Capture

DEFINITION

Media Capture is the state-sponsored hostile takeover of the information ecosystem. Unlike censorship, which seeks only to silence dissent, this tactic aims to conscript the press into the service of the regime. The autocrat recognizes that independent journalism is a structural threat because facts are stubborn rivals to political will. Therefore, the strategy shifts from suppression to ownership. Independent outlets are strangled by regulatory harassment, acquired by regime-aligned oligarchs, or bankrupted by spurious "tax investigations" and libel suits. These hollowed-out institutions are then replaced by a "zombie press." News outlets retain the respected names and high-budget studios of legacy media but function exclusively as public relations firms for the state, wrapping propaganda in the aesthetics of objective news.

EXAMPLE

A legacy media giant, weakened by debt, is acquired by a billionaire with deep familial or financial ties to the ruling elite. Overnight, the network stops investigating the regime and starts promoting it. Failures vanish from the chyron, and reporting shifts toward a sophisticated mix of light entertainment and state praise. To maintain the illusion of objectivity, the network invites token critics from the opposition. These are safe, managed voices who are allowed to speak just enough to validate the channel's independence, but never enough to damage the regime. The audience sees the same trusted anchors and logos, unaware that the network has transitioned from a check on power to its subtlest defender.

TELLTALE SIGNS OF MEDIA CAPTURE

The "White Knight" Acquisition

Media capture rarely begins with soldiers in the newsroom. More often it begins with a merger. A distressed independent outlet is purchased by a business tycoon with lucrative ties to the state. The acquisition is sold as a financial rescue or "strategic pivot," but it is immediately followed by the quiet dismissal or "resignation" of investigative journalists and the installation of management sympathetic to the regime.

Asymmetric Scrutiny

Captured media does not necessarily stop reporting news. It simply applies different standards of evidence. The regime's failures are excused as bad luck or ignored entirely ("bias by omission"), while the opposition's minor gaffes are treated as disqualifying scandals. If a network dedicates investigative resources exclusively to the regime's rivals while reprinting state press releases as fact, it has been captured.

The "Time-Loop" Deflection

A captured outlet actively distracts from current abuses by obsessively relitigating the past. When the regime commits a scandal, the network ignores the breaking news to launch a retrospective investigation into a previous administration or a defeated rival. This institutionalized "whataboutism" floods the information zone with historical grievances, ensuring the public is always looking backward at the "enemy" rather than forward at the leader.

CITIZEN COUNTERMEASURES

Divesting from the Captured Entity

Treating attention as a financial asset is the primary lever of resistance. This involves the cancellation of subscriptions and pressuring local affiliates to drop captured programming, depriving the new owners of the revenue and user data needed to sustain operations. Organized consumer campaigns that target the outlet's advertisers create a "brand safety" crisis, making the cost of carrying regime propaganda financially unsustainable for the parent company.

Finding Better Sources

Reliance on legacy institutions creates vulnerability to capture. The antidote is a distributed trust network. Trust is rebuilt by shifting financial support to independent, subscription-based journalists and local news cooperatives that rely on direct reader funding rather than corporate ownership. Diversifying information sources creates a resilient mesh network of reporting that cannot be silenced by a single acquisition or boardroom purge.

Devaluing the Co-Opted Brand

The regime acquires legacy media specifically to exploit its accumulated prestige. The most effective counter is to strip that asset of its dignity. Relentless mockery, using memes, derisive nicknames, and viral "before-and-after" clips, pierces the aura of authority faster than dry criticism. By reducing a once-respected newsroom to a punchline, citizens destroy the specific value the regime sought to acquire: credibility.

READADJUSTMENTS BEGIN TODAY
THEY'RE CUTTING OUR DINNER RATIONS AGAIN.
THEY'RE JUST READJUSTMENTS.

Newspeak

DEFINITION

Newspeak is the intentional manipulation of language to limit the capacity for critical thought. Originating in George Orwell's *1984*, the tactic relies on a simple premise: if you control the words, you control the minds. By enforcing a simplified vocabulary and removing the tools for complex reasoning, the regime makes it difficult to criticize power. Words are stripped of nuance, inverted, or destroyed entirely. Repression becomes "security," plunder becomes "nationalization," and lies become "alternative facts." The goal is to make independent thought impossible. If the words for freedom or rebellion no longer exist, the concepts themselves wither, leaving citizens with no way to challenge the state.

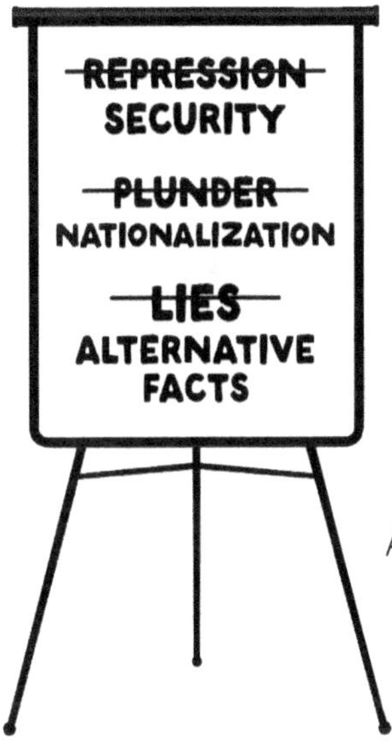

EXAMPLE

A regime sterilizes public discourse by enforcing a vocabulary of sterilized euphemisms. Complex human realities are compressed into rigid blocks that obscure their true nature. A military invasion is categorized as a "Special Law Enforcement Operation"; torture is sanitized as "EITs" (Enhanced Interrogation Techniques); mass deportations become "Resettlements." These euphemisms are designed to be easily spoken but emotionally inert, stripping the acts of their visceral horror. By forcing the population to speak in such sterile administrative terms, the regime severs the link between words and the reality they describe. And without the words, the thoughts themselves become impossible.

TELLTALE SIGNS OF NEWSPEAK

Clinical Euphemisms

The regime replaces visceral words with sterile, medicalized terminology to numb the public's moral response. Instead of admitting to "civilian deaths," official reports cite "collateral damage"; "mass deportation" becomes "administrative transfer." This linguistic distancing acts as an emotional anesthetic, allowing the state to describe human suffering as if it were a routine logistical procedure.

Antonymic Labeling

Laws and agencies are named the exact opposite of their actual function. A bill loosening environmental protections is titled the "Clear Skies Initiative"; a decree expanding surveillance is called the "Freedom Act." By cloaking repressive measures in virtuous titles, the regime forces opponents into the rhetorical trap of appearing to attack "freedom" or "clean skies" itself.

Thought-Terminating Clichés

Nuanced debate is replaced by short, rhythmic slogans designed to stop thinking. Complex crises are dismissed with totalizing phrases like "fake news," "enemies of the people," or "trust the plan." These verbal reflexes serve as stop-signs for the mind, allowing supporters to bypass critical analysis and immediately categorize any dissenting information as a hostile attack.

CITIZEN COUNTERMEASURES

Matching Photos to Labels

Since Newspeak relies on abstraction to hide violence, neutralization is achieved by pairing the sterile official term with photographic evidence of its results. When the state describes a crackdown as "public order maintenance," activists circulate images of the actual police brutality alongside the phrase. This visual context destroys the euphemism's power, preventing the public from accepting the clean label for a dirty reality.

Using Real Words

The private use of descriptive plain-language terms prevents the regime's jargon from monopolizing thought. If the state mandates "security measures," the intentional use of the term "surveillance" serves to maintain a cognitive firewall. This preserves the ability to see the reality that the state attempts to obscure. By keeping the "forbidden" words in circulation, communities ensure the concepts behind them survive.

Staying Silent Loudly

When specific words are banned, citizens switch to a "null" symbol that signifies the censorship itself. For example, holding up blank sheets of paper in public squares. Everyone knows what is "written" on the invisible page, but the regime is paralyzed because it cannot arrest people for holding nothing. It forces the state to ban common objects, making the repression visibly ridiculous.

THE BATTLE OF COWSHED
HISTORIC SITE
SNOWBALL
TRAITOR
~~ANIMAL HERO~~
FIRST CLASS
BOXER
LOSER
~~ANIMAL HERO~~
FIRST CLASS

Rewriting History

DEFINITION

Rewriting History is the authoritarian tactic of replacing documented events with a state-approved version of the past. The goal is to eliminate any memory that threatens the regime and shape public understanding so that the official story becomes the only story people know. This practice relies on the systematic replacement of documentation with state-approved narratives. When archives are altered, textbooks rewritten, search engines filtered, and public discussion criminalized, history becomes a tool of power rather than a record of lived reality. By controlling the narrative of what was, the regime dictates the boundaries of what can be, foreclosing any alternative future. What cannot be remembered cannot be questioned, and what cannot be questioned cannot be resisted.

EXAMPLE

A government responds to a mass protest with lethal force, killing unarmed civilians and suppressing the movement. In the aftermath, officials ban all discussion of the event and remove references from newspapers, school curricula, and public memorials. Search engines within the country return no results for the event. Images and videos disappear from local networks. Even foreign websites and AI systems are filtered so that the incident cannot be queried without triggering surveillance alerts. Citizens who attempt to gather information or commemorate the victims are questioned, detained, or publicly shamed. Over time, a generation grows up with no knowledge of what occurred.

TELLTALE SIGNS OF REWRITING HISTORY

Systematic Erasure of Documentation and Archives
The primary sign is the physical and digital eradication of the original record. The regime alters key archives, bans original textbooks, and digitally filters search engines, AI, and local networks to ensure zero results for sensitive events. This action makes the suppressed event unknowable to the public and future researchers by removing all material sources of truth.

Criminalization and Surveillance of Private Memory
The regime criminalizes discussion, commemoration, and information-gathering about suppressed historical figures and events. Citizens who query sensitive terms or share foreign information are questioned or publicly shamed. This state action makes the sharing of dissenting historical memory a punishable offense, forcing the populace into widespread self-censorship.

Imposing a Singular, Mandatory Narrative in Education
The regime mandates the unchallengeable insertion of the state-approved narrative into all public school curricula. This is replacing the historical record with a simplified official story that justifies the regime's power and existence. The goal is to ensure that a new generation grows up with no organic knowledge of the suppressed truth.

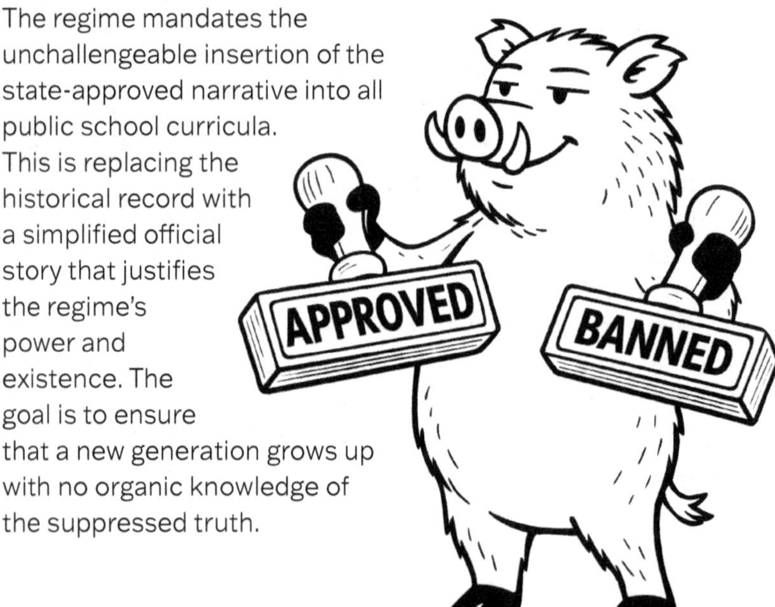

CITIZEN COUNTERMEASURES

Saving the Files

Digitally archiving and distributing primary sources related to suppressed figures and events is a foundational safeguard. Uploading original documents, photos, and testimony to decentralized international platforms creates necessary redundancy. This process of "memory banking" ensures that the physical destruction of archives inside the country does not lead to the total erasure of history.

Teaching the Truth

Countering the singular state narrative by establishing informal networks for historical education relies on the cumulative power of distributed groups. While sometimes precarious and requiring discretion, the organization of private study groups and sharing of banned articles creates a resilient alternative to the formal school system. This ensures the rising generation receives the complete historical record, effectively breaking the regime's monopoly on the national narrative.

Telling the World

The role of witness multiplier is to share verified histories with international institutions. This transforms individual memories into public facts. Getting suppressed events validated and published abroad creates an external repository of truth. This provides a political shield, making it significantly harder for the regime to deny history without damaging its international standing.

WHO SHOULD WE TRUST?
THIS IS WHAT THE DATA SHOW.
WELL, THAT'S JUST YOUR OPINION.
DR. MILLER
MELVIN

War on Expertise

DEFINITION

The War on Expertise is the deliberate campaign to discredit independent knowledge institutions because they serve objective truth rather than the state. Because their professional standards demand loyalty to evidence over authority, the regime views academics, scientists, journalists, and doctors as threats to its control. To politically taint them, the leadership rebrands their work as a partisan conspiracy. By spinning inconvenient perspectives as "elitist" and contrary evidence as "rigged," the regime attempts to immunize itself against inconvenient truths. When the referees are discredited, the leader removes the only objective check on their power, securing the impunity to govern without limits.

EXAMPLE

A nation's economy runs on fossil fuels. When scientists prove that burning these fuels is destabilizing the climate, the energy giants face an existential threat. To protect their profits, they pour massive funding into the regime, effectively purchasing a policy of denial. The government, serving its donors rather than the public, attacks the messengers. Research funding is cut, and climatologists are branded as "alarmist" and "anti-growth" traitors. To confuse the public, state media put fringe pundits on screen next to serious scientists, pretending they have equal standing. The goal isn't to disprove the science, but to create enough doubt to delay action. By turning a physics problem into a culture war, the regime ensures the industry's profits keep flowing while the planet burns.

TELLTALE SIGNS OF WAR ON EXPERTISE

False Equivalence

The regime or its media allies regularly present fringe contrarians alongside established experts to simulate a balanced debate. By giving a lone skeptic the same airtime and visual weight as a representative of the scientific consensus, they create the illusion that the facts are contested. This confuses the public, making settled science appear to be a matter of "open opinion."

Ad Hominem Attacks

Instead of engaging with the evidence, state actors attack the researchers' character or class. Experts are "wrong" precisely because they are "elites," "globalists," or "funded by the opposition." This rhetorical shift turns education into a vice, citing the possession of specialized knowledge as evidence of disloyalty to the "common man" and the state.

The Rise of Parallel Institutions

The state creates or elevates pseudo-academic organizations to produce "alternative facts." These entities mimic the aesthetics of expertise, using titles, journals, and conferences, but exist solely to validate regime policy. By flooding the zone with this pseudoscience, the government dilutes the authority of legitimate institutions, making it impossible for the average citizen to discern credible sources.

CITIZEN COUNTERMEASURES

Mapping the Conflict of Interest

Since the regime elevates "counter-experts" to feign debate, resistance involves exposing their financial incentives rather than debating their claims. Activists use Open Source Intelligence (OSINT) to trace and visualize the funding streams connecting these pundits to state-aligned industries. Revealing the transaction discredits the source, shifting the public perception of their arguments from "scientific skepticism" to "paid lobbying."

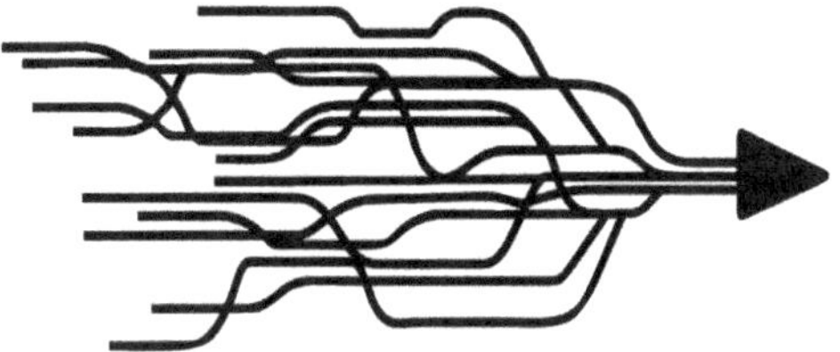

Talking to the Source

To bypass state-mediated distortions, communities create direct lines of communication with verified experts. This involves the organization of local "teach-ins" or encrypted digital forums where scientists and professionals can share findings directly with citizens, bypassing government filters. By removing the regime as the informational middleman, communities re-anchor their decision-making in primary source expertise rather than the state's curated interpretation.

Mirroring Vulnerable Databases

When the regime attempts to scrub inconvenient data (e.g., climate or health statistics), citizen archiving provides a redundant backup system. Using tools like the Internet Archive or decentralized storage protocols (IPFS), individuals download and mirror at-risk public datasets before they are purged. This strategy prevents the state from rewriting history by deletion and preserves the original empirical record for future accountability and analysis.

STAGE III

The Mechanics of Control

Whether whispering from the shadows of the throne or standing newly crowned upon it, the *Tyrannus Rex* has now crossed the threshold from meddlesome operative to existential threat. With the reins of power seized, the machinery must now be built. The creature cannot hunt everywhere at once, so it constructs a nervous system of surveillance and bureaucracy to enforce its will. This stage analyzes the "hardware" of the new order: the conversion of free citizens into manageable subjects. The chaotic energy of the movement calcifies into the cold efficiency of a machine designed for self-preservation. To resist, we must understand the architecture of our capture. Drawing from the blueprints of coercion, we isolate ten instruments of force to find the flaws in the design. We map the leverage. We trace the wires. We jam the mechanics to break the chains.

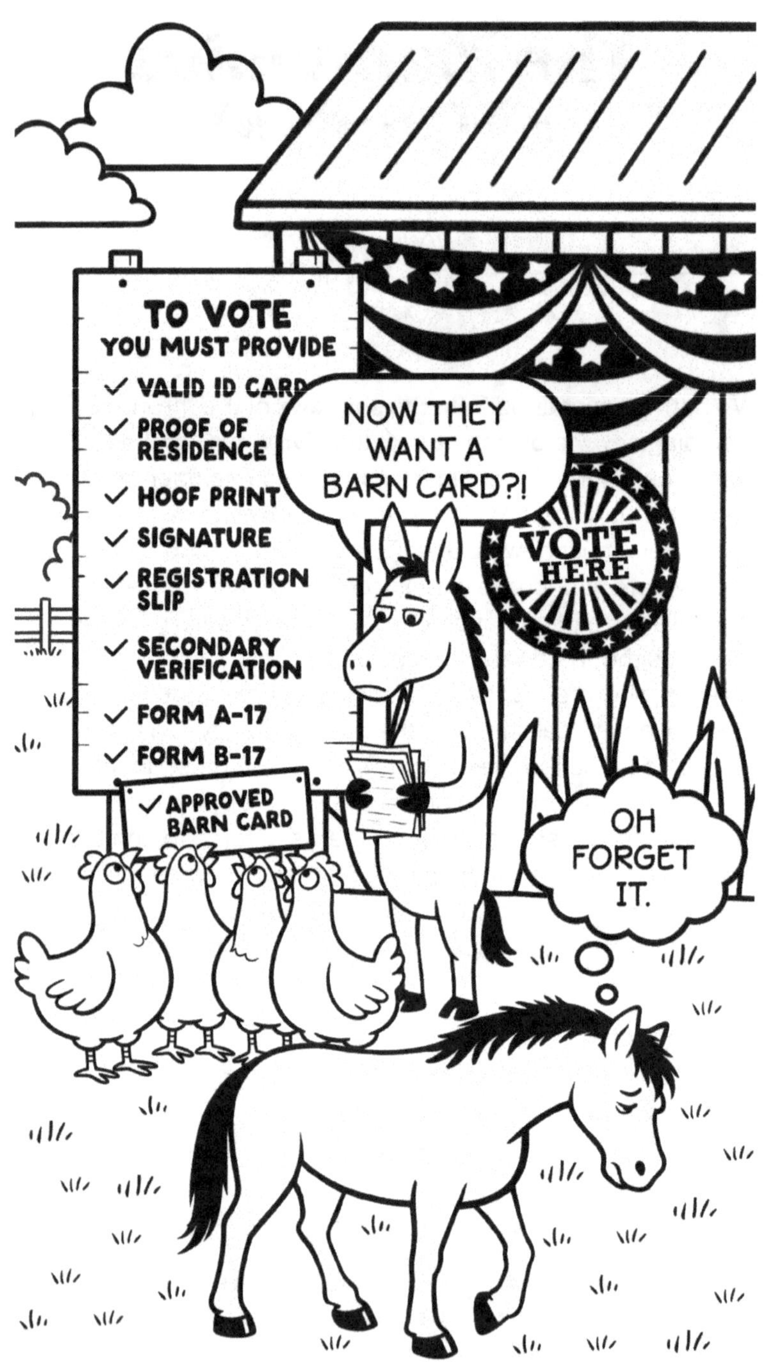
TO VOTE
YOU MUST PROVIDE
✓ VALID ID CARD
✓ PROOF OF RESIDENCE
✓ HOOF PRINT
✓ SIGNATURE
✓ REGISTRATION SLIP
✓ SECONDARY VERIFICATION
✓ FORM A-17
✓ FORM B-17
✓ APPROVED BARN CARD
NOW THEY WANT A BARN CARD?!
VOTE HERE
OH FORGET IT.

Apathy Trap

DEFINITION

The Apathy Trap is the deliberate induction of learned helplessness to drain citizens of the will to act. Unlike traditional totalitarianism, which demands fanatical loyalty, this strategy relies on exhaustion and cynicism. The regime ensures that scandals pile up without consequence and institutions fail without repair, teaching the public that outrage is a finite resource with zero return on investment. Bureaucratic sludge compounds the effect: voting is made needlessly difficult, benefits are buried in labyrinthine forms, and complaints disappear into administrative voids. The goal is to convince citizens that the system is corrupt and that engagement is a waste of time. When the effort of participation exceeds the reward, citizens stop trying. That is not a side effect. That is the objective.

EXAMPLE

A regime maintains the rituals of voting while simultaneously discouraging participation. Complex registration rules, workday elections, and gerrymandered districts make casting a ballot physically difficult and mathematically meaningless. Meanwhile, a pervasive narrative insists that "the system is rigged" and "both sides are the same." Then, the hammer drops. To neutralize opposition strongholds, the regime in power suspends voting in targeted swing districts, citing "corruption" or "irregularities." Military or paramilitary units are deployed to "secure" polling stations. Seeing that the machinery of the election is rigged and the environment is hostile, the average citizen calculates that the cost of participation outweighs the hope of change and stays home.

TELLTALE SIGNS OF APATHY TRAP

Bureaucratic Sludge

The state intentionally makes essential processes like voting, accessing benefits, or filing complaints convoluted. By using complex forms and opaque rules, the regime ensures that engagement requires an exhausting amount of time and energy. This "sludge" acts as a friction filter, disenfranchising the majority without formally banning participation, as citizens simply give up in frustration.

Performative Incompetence

The government displays a calculated inability to solve solvable problems, treating chronic failures like power outages or uncollected trash as unfixable "facts of life." Officials shrug off crises with feigned helplessness. This constant, low-level dysfunction lowers public expectations, training citizens to believe that competent government is impossible. If the system is perceived as inherently broken, demanding better governance feels like a waste of energy.

The "Universal Corruption" Narrative

State rhetoric shifts from defending the leader to insisting that everyone is corrupt. Propaganda promotes the idea that all politicians are liars and all systems are rigged ("they are all the same"). By convincing the public that the alternative is just as bad as the status quo, the regime prevents moral outrage. If change brings no improvement, the incentive to mobilize vanishes.

CITIZEN COUNTERMEASURES

Cutting the Red Tape

To counter the "sludge" designed to exhaust voters, support groups are created to lower the barriers to participation. This involves organizing "form-filling parties," creating how-to videos for complex regulations, and establishing mutual-aid transportation networks to bypass physical barriers. This absorption of the administrative burden on behalf of the vulnerable serves to negate the state's strategy of disenfranchisement through exhaustion.

Showing it Works Elsewhere

To dismantle the narrative that dysfunction is inevitable, activists circulate evidence of functioning systems in other jurisdictions. By presenting concrete case studies of successful models abroad, it becomes clear that the regime's failures are political choices, not inevitabilities. This "proof of possibility" pierces the bubble of cynicism, replacing the belief that "nothing works" with the demand for specific, proven alternatives.

Winning Small Battles

To reverse learned helplessness, communities shift focus from unmovable national issues to winnable local battles, such as repairing infrastructure or staffing a school board. Achieving a concrete, visible result, however small, provides empirical proof that action produces change. These "efficacy loops" retrain the citizen's brain to reject cynicism and rebuild the collective confidence necessary to eventually challenge the regime on national issues.

DONKEY
WORK COUNCIL
MEETING
TONIGHT
SHIFT
SCHEDULES
DISCUSSION
COUNCIL
PROHIBITED
Questions
About Your
Schedule?
REPORT
TO FERN
FERN

Atomization

DEFINITION

Between the citizen and the state stand unions, professional associations, and neighborhood councils. Atomization is the strategic dismantling of every one of them, until the individual stands alone. This fragmentation prevents citizens from pooling their resources or validating their grievances, transforming a cohesive public into a collection of vulnerable individuals. By destroying these "buffer zones" of civil society, the regime effectively eliminates the only mechanism capable of challenging its power. The ultimate goal is to break the horizontal bonds of trust between citizens, leaving only the vertical bond of submission to the leader. In this vacuum, resistance is not just dangerous; it is structurally impossible, as there is no "we" left to resist, only a collection of isolated, terrified "I"s.

IT'S SO MUCH HARDER WITHOUT A "WE."

EXAMPLE

A regime facing economic unrest dismantles trade unions but simultaneously launches a high-efficiency "citizen complaint" app. If a worker has a wage dispute, they can file an individual ticket and get a swift resolution from the state. However, if that same worker attempts to organize a meeting with colleagues to discuss collective wages, they are arrested for "disturbing the peace." The message is clear: the state will care for you as a dependent subject, but it will crush you as an organized class. By using public services to reward isolation and punish solidarity, the regime ensures that citizens remain vertically connected to power but horizontally estranged from one another.

TELLTALE SIGNS OF ATOMIZATION

The Criminalization of Association

The state redefines private, voluntary gatherings as potential threats to public order. Seemingly apolitical groups like book clubs, hobbyist leagues, or parent-teacher associations are subjected to burdensome registration laws or outright bans. This legal pressure forces citizens to abandon group activities, not because they are illegal per se, but because the regulatory risk of gathering makes isolation the safer choice.

Centralizing Grievance

The regime dismantles lateral communication channels (unions, neighborhood councils) and replaces them with direct, individual lines to the state. Citizens are encouraged to solve problems by petitioning the leader or reporting their neighbors via apps or hotlines, rather than organizing collectively. This "hub-and-spoke" structure ensures that while the state hears every complaint, citizens never hear each other, preventing the formation of shared solidarity.

The Erosion of Social Trust

A pervasive culture of suspicion replaces community cohesion. Through the widespread use of informants or the public shaming of "disloyal" elements, the regime incentivizes citizens to monitor one another. When people fear that their neighbor, colleague, or family member might report them for a private comment, they self-censor and withdraw from genuine social interaction. The result is a society of individuals who share physical space but inhabit private psychological bunkers.

CITIZEN COUNTERMEASURES

Sending Secret Signals

To shatter the illusion of isolation, resistance movements coordinate low-stakes, high-visibility actions, such as wearing a specific color, banging pots at a set hour, or turning off lights simultaneously. These rituals allow atomized individuals to visualize the true extent of shared dissent without exposing themselves to the risks of a physical protest. The sudden visual or auditory confirmation that "I am not alone" breaks the psychological hold of the regime.

Helping Each Other

To break the "divide and conquer" leverage of the state, communities provide decentralized support systems like food distribution, childcare co-ops, or emergency funds that operate outside government channels. Such networks reduce individual reliance on state services and act as "solidarity drills." The practical experience of reciprocal care proves to isolated citizens that a community still exists and is capable of solving problems independently.

Meeting Under Cover

To circumvent bans on political organizing, people re-connect through seemingly benign activities like book clubs, hiking groups, or religious study. These "cover" organizations rebuild trust and social capital without triggering immediate state repression. By normalizing face-to-face interaction in non-political contexts, communities repair the horizontal networks necessary for future collective action, effectively regrowing the buffer zones the state attempted to destroy.

VOTE
TODAY
CANCELED
GRAND MILITARY PARADE
TODAY

Bread and Circuses

DEFINITION

Bread and Circuses (*panem et circenses*) is the strategic trading of political liberty for material comfort and spectacle. Originating from the Roman poet Juvenal, the tactic describes how autocrats soothe civic unrest by providing basic subsistence ("bread") and mass entertainment ("circuses") while they dismantle democratic institutions. In its modern form, the regime replaces structural reform with performative charity. Direct payments and subsidies are branded as personal gifts from the leader, while state-sponsored sports and media spectacles occupy the cognitive space where political debate should exist. The goal is to infantilize the population, keeping them fed and entertained such that they lack the hunger or the focus to demand accountability.

EXAMPLE

When an authoritarian faces criticism over governance failures or institutional decay, they attempt to buy their way out of trouble. The leader authorizes direct cash payments or material benefits, ensuring that every check or package carries their personal signature or likeness. This markets public relief as a private gift from the ruler rather than a state entitlement. Simultaneously, the regime floods the calendar with sporting events, military parades, or nationalist concerts, saturated with patriotic imagery. The media narrative shifts entirely to these celebrations, drowning out dissent and policy critiques. The public is incentivized to cheer and consume rather than question, effectively replacing civic engagement with transactional support.

TELLTALE SIGNS OF BREAD AND CIRCUSES

Sportswashing

The regime prioritizes high-visibility spectacles over governance. They aggressively bid for mega-events like the Olympics or purchase global sports teams while domestic services crumble. These events generate a nationalist "sugar high" that temporarily overrides economic grievance. Simultaneously, they launder the regime's reputation on the global stage, making international criticism difficult during the festivities.

Renting the Celebrity Class

The regime builds a patronage network that rewards prominent athletes and celebrities with exclusive state privileges in exchange for conspicuous allegiance. While these figures often possess independent fame, their continued access to power and privilege becomes tied to the leader's favor. The state effectively trades political protection for cultural capital. In moments of crisis, the regime calls upon these beloved figures to stand by the leader, using their popularity to transform a political choice into a cultural one: if your heroes have chosen the regime, perhaps you should too.

The Branded Handout

In a democracy, welfare is institutional; in an autocracy, it is personal. The regime brands food baskets, medicine, or stimulus checks with the leader's name or likeness. This psychological trick co-opts public funds for acts of "private benevolence." It conditions citizens to view their very survival as a gift granted to them by the ruler.

CITIZEN COUNTERMEASURES

Naming the Real Cost

Successful movements have tarnished the glamour of the "circus" by translating the cost of military parades, mega-events, or lavish festivals into specific, relatable losses. By sharing data that equates the budget of a single spectacle to the cost of unfunded hospitals or schools, opposition groups turn opulent displays into monuments of theft and vanity. This approach helps the public see the "circus" for what it is: an expensive, manipulative distraction.

PARADE BILL

Flags
Street Closures
Security
New Uniforms
Confetti

TOTAL
5,600
Bags of Grain

Crashing the Party

Regimes rely on sports and entertainment venues being "neutral" zones where dissent is socially unacceptable. Counter-movements have broken this spell by staging visible protests inside the venue or chanting during live broadcasts. This tactic forces the state to use censorship or police force during a celebration, thereby denying the dictator the propaganda victory of a unified, adoring crowd.

Cashing the Check, Keeping the Vote

To counter the psychological leverage of branded handouts, opposition groups decouple the material benefit from the expected loyalty. Rather than stigmatizing the recipients who often need the aid to survive, activists highlight the regime's cynical assumption that citizens can be bought. By characterizing the "gift" as a manipulative bribe that insults the public's integrity, this narrative shifts the shame onto the giver. The resulting strategy encourages pragmatic defiance: citizens feel empowered to accept the resources as their due ("Take the gift, it's yours"), while refusing to deliver the political support the regime expects in return.

PROTECT
BARNYARD VALUES
THAT WON'T FLY HERE. WE HAVE VALUES.

Coded Signaling

DEFINITION

Coded Signaling is the strategic use of words or phrases that carry a distinct, exclusionary meaning for an in-group while remaining deniable to outsiders. Commonly known as "dog whistles," these signals function as a dual-frequency communication channel: on the surface, they appear neutral or patriotic, but underneath they convey radical solidarity or hostility. This duality allows the speaker to evade accountability while supporters hear the message clearly. Phrases like "states' rights," "cosmopolitan," or "from the river to the sea" act as social passwords within their groups, marking who belongs and who is the enemy. Over time, repetition dulls the disguise. What begins as coded language often hardens into overt slogans, turning whistles into bullhorns.

EXAMPLE

A politician running on a platform of "restoring traditional values" repeatedly references a specific historical date or obscure slogan. This reference acts as a prism, splitting the audience into two distinct realities. To the general public, it sounds like a nostalgic throwaway line. To the extremist fringe, however, it is a precise reference to a past regime or a violent uprising. When journalists point out the connection, the politician feigns ignorance and accuses the media of "reading too much into it." Meanwhile, the fringe base is energized, having received confirmation that the leader shares their worldview but is too savvy to say it out loud. The signal has been received, and the plausible deniability remains intact.

TELLTALE SIGNS OF CODED SIGNALING

Strategic Ambiguity

The speaker consistently uses terms that have a benign dictionary definition but a loaded political history. When challenged, they retreat to the literal meaning (e.g., claiming "states' rights" is merely about constitutional law), accusing critics of paranoia. This forced ambiguity allows them to court extremists without alienating moderates, creating a shield of plausible deniability against accusations of bigotry.

The Reaction Gap

The coded message produces sharply divided reactions that seem disproportionate to the literal words spoken. The in-group hears the dog whistle and responds with intense enthusiasm or mobilization, while the out-group remains confused or indifferent. If a seemingly dry policy speech triggers raucous applause or knowing nods from a radical faction, the speaker likely signaled a specific ideological alignment.

Semantic Incongruity

The speaker uses oddly specific, antiquated, or jarringly precise language where a standard term would suffice. Instead of saying "bankers," they say "international financiers"; instead of "crime," they say "urban decay." These linguistic choices are not accidental stylistic quirks. They are passwords designed to signal fluency in a radical ideology while maintaining a veneer of polite political discourse.

CITIZEN COUNTERMEASURES

Asking for Details

To expose the hidden exclusionary intent, citizens and journalists adopt a strategy of "naive" literalism, asking the speaker to explain the specific mechanics of their coded phrase in agonizing detail. (e.g., "Which specific 'globalists' are you referring to, and what banks do they run?"). By treating the code as a serious policy statement rather than a rhetorical flourish, the questioner forces the speaker to either retreat into incoherence or reveal the prejudice underlying the term.

Decoding the Signals

To nullify the advantage of ambiguity, civil society groups create and distribute "translation guides" that map coded terms to their extremist origins and intended meanings. By explicitly linking a benign-sounding phrase (e.g., "cultural Marxism") to its specific historical baggage (e.g., antisemitic conspiracy theories), citizens strip away the plausible deniability. This forces the speaker to either abandon the code or openly defend the radical ideology it conceals.

Watching the Crowd

When a public figure uses a dog whistle, resistance involves flooding the information space with the immediate context, such as clips of the speaker using the same term in radical settings or endorsements from extremist groups. Instead of debating the literal definition of the word, citizens pivot the conversation to who is cheering. This shifts the burden of proof, forcing the speaker to disavow their most fervent supporters, which fractures their coalition.

ELIMINATE THE INFESTATION
SNOWBALL
IS A SICKNESS
NO TO
SNOWBA
SNOWBALL IS A PLAGUE ON OUR FARM!

Demonization

DEFINITION

Demonization is the portrayal of political opponents and vulnerable groups as inherently evil or sub-human. Rather than contesting ideas, the regime scapegoats minorities or some other convenient social group, blaming them for societal problems to justify stripping their rights. This assault often expands to institutions, branding independent media and the judiciary as "enemies of the people" to weaken accountability. By employing dehumanizing language that labels protesters as "terrorists" and critics as "traitors," the state cultivates a primal "us vs. them" fear. This moral exclusion is strategic: once the "other" is portrayed as a threat to national security or culture, ordinary ethical restraints collapse, and repression is legitimized as self-defense.

EXAMPLE

A demagogue combines biological disgust with spiritual warfare to target a minority group. The regime initially brands these citizens as "vermin" or "parasites," stripping them of human status. However, to justify extreme measures, propaganda introduces a crucial paradox: the "sub-human" is simultaneously depicted as a hyper-capable mastermind controlling the levers of power. This shift transforms the target from a mere nuisance into a diabolical threat. Leaders often co-opt religious or traditional narratives, claiming they are defending the "divine order" against this cunning evil. By promoting the enemy as both a filthy contagion and an omnipotent predator, the state claims that violence is a righteous, defensive act of survival.

TELLTALE SIGNS OF DEMONIZATION

Biological Metaphors

The most distinct warning sign is a shift in rhetoric from political disagreement to biological revulsion. Leaders stop debating policy and start using medical or agricultural metaphors, describing opponents as "vermin," "cancer," "rats," or "filth." This language is designed to trigger the brain's disgust response, bypassing the moral inhibition against harming humans by framing the target as a pathogen that must be "cleansed."

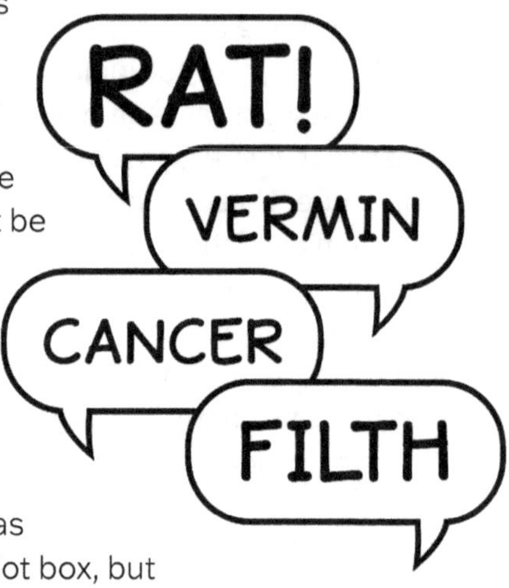

Existential Threats

The regime equates political competition with a battle for physical survival. Opponents are not described as rivals to be defeated at the ballot box, but as "existential threats" bent on destroying the nation's culture or existence. By asserting that "they" are actively plotting to exterminate "us," the state argues that normal rules of law no longer apply and that preemptive violence is necessary self-preservation.

"Hidden Hand" Narratives

Propaganda attributes a secret, omnipotent power to the marginalized group, claiming they control the media, banks, or global events from the shadows. This creates a strategic paradox: the enemy is depicted as culturally "degenerate" (sub-human) yet politically dominant (super-human). By convincing the public that a vulnerable minority is actually a powerful puppet master, the regime portrays its own aggression as a heroic rebellion against a tyrannical "deep state" or cabal.

CITIZEN COUNTERMEASURES

Mixing the Groups

Organizing low-risk, localized interactions between the demonized group and the general public, such as community aid projects or underground cultural exchanges, utilizes the "contact hypothesis" to break social barriers. These controlled environments provide direct empirical evidence that contradicts state-promoted stereotypes. The resulting integration creates a "social shield," where neighbors become less likely to comply with discriminatory directives or remain silent during state-led persecution.

Standing in the Gap

Nothing defeats isolation faster than visible, collective solidarity, the majority adopting the symbols of a demonized group until the demonization has nowhere left to land. When a broad cross-section of the public adopts the "out-group" identifier, it creates a signal-to-noise problem for enforcers and renders the demonization labels socially impotent. This proactive mass-identification forces the regime to either concede its narrative or risk a costly, undifferentiated crackdown on the general population.

Sharing Human Stories

Disseminating mundane, relatable narratives about the marginalized group serves to counteract "othering" narratives. By sharing personal biographies, daily routines, and shared cultural values through decentralized social media or community bulletins, activists disrupt the psychological process of dehumanization. This re-establishes empathetic bonds within the broader populace, raising the social cost for the state to execute repressive actions against the demonized demographic.

SNOWBALL · I AM A PIG

MOBILIZE FOR WAR
WHAT HAPPENED TO ALL THE MISSING GRAIN?

Diversionary War

DEFINITION

A Diversionary War is a manufactured or opportunistically escalated conflict used to redirect public anger away from domestic problems and rally support around the leader. This dynamic is colloquially known as "wagging the dog." In this context, "war" is broadly applied: it may take the form of an actual military operation, a proxy conflict, or a crusade against abstractions such as crime, drugs, corruption, terrorism, or immigration. The key is that the leader chooses conflicts they cannot easily lose and that designate a clear, externalized "other" as the root of all national problems. Instead of the leader being held responsible for policy failures, the nation's energy is channeled into a perceived life-or-death struggle against an enemy.

EXAMPLE

An authoritarian confronts a personal scandal at home. Rather than address the issue, they announce a campaign against a nearby "threat." The enemy is described as a network of traffickers, smugglers, or foreign-backed criminals whose actions endanger national security. A routine maritime encounter is reported as an act of aggression. When a skirmish inevitably occurs—whether through miscommunication, escalation, or orchestration—the leader declares that patience has run out. Critics who question the timing or necessity of the confrontation are accused of siding with criminals and undermining national security. The campaign drags on without clear metrics for success, because its real purpose is to bury a crisis at home.

TELLTALE SIGNS OF DIVERSIONARY WAR

Convenient Crisis Timing

The "war" erupts seemingly out of nowhere at the exact moment the leader or ruling party is facing a severe, unrelated domestic crisis. The new conflict conveniently and immediately shifts the national conversation and media narrative away from the leader's failures and onto an external "threat."

A Vague or Disproportionate Enemy

The chosen enemy is either disproportionately weak (a nation that poses no real, immediate threat) or abstract (a "crusade" against "terror," "drugs," or "corruption"). A weak enemy ensures the leader cannot lose, and an abstract enemy ensures the "war" never has to end. This motive is confirmed when the leader actively rejects opportunities to de-escalate and end the conflict.

Equating Dissent with Treason

The leader and their media allies immediately dismiss all criticism of the new war as betrayal. Any person or group that questions the war's timing or necessity is publicly labeled as "siding with the enemy." This rhetorical tactic is the key mechanism for replacing domestic accountability with national mobilization.

CITIZEN COUNTERMEASURES

Staying on Topic

The strategic purpose of diversionary war is to shift attention from internal failure. Refusing to accept this shift is the primary countermeasure. Linking the high costs and risks of the external conflict directly back to domestic incompetence, whether economic or political, short-circuits the distraction. This persistent focus prevents the regime from burying its failures under the noise of jingoism.

Talking to the "Enemy"

Diversionary aggression relies on dehumanizing an external enemy to increase in-group cohesion. Actively amplifying voices from the targeted group disrupts this narrative. Sharing perspectives and highlighting the human cost on ordinary people counteracts the necessary propaganda. This cross-border dialogue raises the social cost of the conflict by revealing the "other" as a community rather than a threat, undermining the pretext for war.

Denying the "Rally 'Round the Flag" Effect

Authoritarians often initiate conflict solely to harvest the short-term surge in popularity known as the "rally 'round the flag" effect. Differentiating between the nation and the regime is essential. Supporting troops or victims while withholding support for the political leadership prevents the conversion of crisis into legitimacy. This refusal to suspend critical judgment denies the leader the domestic political capital sought through aggression.

PRESS
PRESS
PRESS
PRESS
ARE YOU EVER GOING TO FIX THIS?
INTERESTING QUESTION... PUT THIS ON.
FOREIGN AGENT

Foreign Agent Trap

DEFINITION

The Foreign Agent Trap is the use of deliberately vague laws to silence dissent by rebranding critics as agents of foreign influence. Under these statutes, "political activity" and "foreign influence" are defined so broadly that nearly any NGO, journalist, academic group, or minority-rights organization can be targeted without evidence of wrongdoing. The tactic forces impossible choices: accept the stigmatizing label of "foreign agent" and lose public trust, or refuse and face fines, raids, and closure. The primary goal is to cut off foreign funding for NGOs and independent media that hold power accountable. The predictable result is a chilling effect, as organizations preemptively shut down to avoid persecution.

WHOA!

PRESS

EXAMPLE

An authoritarian government introduces a "foreign agent" law under the banner of transparency. At first it targets NGOs, then expands quietly. Individual journalists, activists, artists, and online creators are added to the registry for receiving foreign funding or expressing political views. The label carries the weight of betrayal, reviving cultural memories of spies and traitors. Public institutions cut ties. Advertisers withdraw. Those designated must file relentless financial disclosures and mark every article, video, or social media post with a warning that they are a "foreign agent." Minor errors trigger fines, frozen accounts, and criminal charges. Facing prison or bankruptcy, many flee the country. In the end, the state no longer needs to silence dissent. The law has done it for them.

TELLTALE SIGNS OF FOREIGN AGENT TRAP

Nationalistic Rhetoric
Legislation is introduced under the guise of protecting the state from "external interference" or "neocolonialism." The regime claims a free press and NGOs are Trojan horses for foreign interests, shifting the public focus from the content of the dissent to the source of the funding. This narrative creates a patriotic pretext for dismantling democratic checks and balances under the banner of security.

Intentionally Vague Definitions
The legal text employs overly broad language, defining "political activity" as any action intended to influence public opinion or government policy. By refusing to clarify what constitutes "influence," the state grants itself total discretionary power. This ambiguity ensures that no organization can ever be fully compliant, leaving every independent entity in a state of permanent legal vulnerability and self-censorship.

Stigmatizing Self-Labeling
A hallmark sign is the requirement for organizations to proactively label their own communications with derogatory descriptors, such as "foreign agent" or "organization performing the functions of a foreign representative." This mechanism is designed to poison the well of public trust, effectively forcing activists to participate in their own social marginalization and branding their output as inherently suspicious before it is even read.

CITIZEN COUNTERMEASURES

Wearing the Label Proudly

The "Foreign Agent" label is worn as a badge of civic integrity rather than a mark of shame. By publicly endorsing and volunteering for targeted groups, community members absorb the social stigma and dilute the label's potency. When ordinary people openly identify with the "agent," the state's attempt to "other" the dissidents fails to gain psychological traction

Funding Person to Person

Transitioning from institutional grants to "micro-donorship" involves individuals setting up recurring, small-scale transfers to local organizers through non-institutional channels. By bypassing formal NGO bank accounts and using cash-based mutual aid or local credit unions, citizens render the "foreign funding" metric irrelevant. This creates a financially resilient network that is statistically impossible for the state to characterize as a single "foreign-led" entity, grounding the movement in domestic reality.

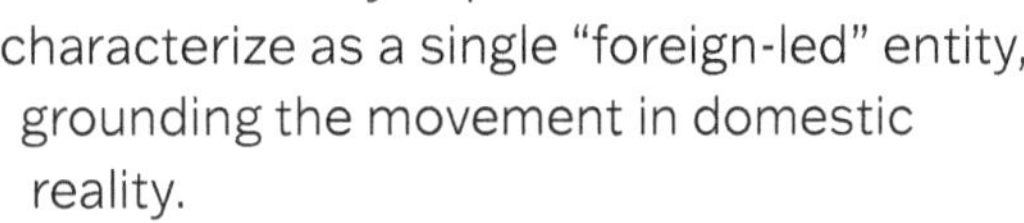

Clogging the System

Legal inquiries are used to create massive administrative backlogs. By demanding individual clarifications on every vague provision of the law, citizens launch a "paperwork strike" that consumes state enforcement resources while simultaneously providing a legal shield for targeted organizations. The regime must choose between processing an avalanche of paperwork and actually governing. It cannot do both.

REPORT SUSPICIOUS ACTIVITY
EARN EXTRA GRAIN
INSERT TIPS HERE
WHY ARE THEY LOOKING AT ME?

Informant Systems

DEFINITION

Informant Systems are the use of peer surveillance to silence dissent by turning citizens into instruments of state monitoring. Rather than relying solely on police or intelligence services, the regime recruits ordinary people to watch one another. Neighbors, coworkers, students, clergy, and family members are encouraged or coerced to report speech, associations, and attitudes deemed disloyal. The objective is both comprehensive intelligence and social corrosion. When anyone might be an informant, trust becomes a liability and any sense of privacy evaporates. People learn to censor themselves long before the state intervenes. The system works precisely because it feels informal and omnipresent, making fear routine and resistance impossible to coordinate.

EXAMPLE

A government announces a new public safety initiative encouraging citizens to report "unpatriotic activity." An anonymous hotline and mobile app are launched, promising confidentiality and cash rewards for tips that lead to enforcement action. Officials emphasize civic duty, but the incentive is clear: verified reports can earn payments equivalent to a month's wages. Almost immediately, reporting spikes. Neighbors submit photos of gatherings, overheard conversations, and social media posts. Workplace disputes and personal grudges are weaponized, with citizens using the reporting system to settle scores and punish rivals. Trust erodes rapidly. The system conditions citizens to police themselves, and each other, for profit and survival.

TELLTALE SIGNS OF INFORMANT SYSTEMS

Incentivizing Minor Civil Reporting

The state introduces rewards for reporting "suspicious" behavior or "unpatriotic" speech among peers. This mechanism encourages citizens to view their neighbors as potential sources of personal gain. By monetizing or incentivizing surveillance, the regime successfully recruits a massive, self-sustaining workforce of civilian monitors without expanding the formal police budget.

Normalizing National Loyalty Oaths

Authorities mandate frequent, public declarations of loyalty. These requirements force individuals to constantly signal their alignment with the state. This environment makes anyone who remains silent or neutral appear suspicious, compelling peers to report them to avoid being accused of complicity or shared "disloyalty."

Expanding Local Security Committees

The government establishes neighborhood-level committees or "volunteer" safety groups that operate outside of standard legal oversight. These groups are granted vague authority to monitor residents and maintain "public order." Their presence ensures constant, local-level observation, making it impossible for citizens to move or communicate freely without being noticed by someone with a direct line to state authorities.

CITIZEN COUNTERMEASURES

Drowning the Hotline

The generation of high volumes of "junk" data regarding mundane activities, such as grocery shopping habits or neighborhood walks, serves to overwhelm state analysts. This tactical noise makes it impossible for authorities to distinguish between routine behavior and actual resistance. The resulting administrative backlog consumes state resources and reduces the predictive value of civilian-sourced intelligence.

INSERT TIPS HERE

Freezing Out Spies

Establishing a community standard where cooperation with state surveillance leads to immediate social ostracization raises the cost of informing. When individuals who provide information to authorities face a total loss of community status and support, the recruitment of new spies becomes more difficult. This community standard of non-cooperation starves the state of human intelligence by isolating those who facilitate its monitoring.

Using Safety Codes

Coded signals are used to confirm a setting is secure before engaging in sensitive dialogue. These signals, such as the specific placement of a household object or a standardized greeting, act as a "go/no-go" gauge for the current threat level. By limiting information exchange to those who recognize these signals, groups ensure that informants are excluded from hearing compromising information.

STOP! THEY'RE ALWAYS WATCHING!

Panopticon

DEFINITION

The Panopticon is a strategy of control that relies on pervasive, integrated surveillance to induce obedience through the fear of observation. Named after Jeremy Bentham's prison design where inmates could be watched at any moment but could never see the watcher, the modern panopticon is digital and omnipresent. Regimes fuse data from financial records, social media, biometrics, video surveillance, travel logs, and smart devices into a single "god view" of the citizen. The strategic goal is less about law enforcement and more about self-censorship. When citizens believe that any transgression might be flagged, they police themselves more effectively than any secret police force ever could. Ultimately, the citizen becomes their own warden, enforcing the regime's rules from within.

BUT...THEY'RE JUST GOOFING AROUND.

EXAMPLE

A regime weaponizes the very devices citizens rely on for daily life. The state deploys military-grade spyware capable of infiltrating smartphones without the user ever clicking a suspicious link. Once infected, the device is transformed into a roving surveillance unit: intelligence agencies can bypass encryption to read private messages, track real-time locations, and remotely activate microphones and cameras to record face-to-face conversations. This capability targets the central nervous system of civil society: trust. When critics know that their most intimate discussions could be streaming to a government server, sources go silent, coordination becomes impossible, and the resistance effectively dismantles itself out of fear.

TELLTALE SIGNS OF PANOPTICON

The "Super-ID" Consolidation

The state introduces a unified digital identity system that merges disparate data silos. Initially marketed as convenience for tax filing or healthcare, it rapidly becomes mandatory for buying SIM cards, accessing banking, or boarding trains. When a single government portal links your financial survival to your internet activity and physical location, the infrastructure for total control is complete.

The Biometric Dragnet

Surveillance expands from tracking devices to tracking biology. "Smart City" initiatives roll out cameras equipped with facial recognition on street corners, while mandatory biometric registration (fingerprints, iris scans, or DNA) becomes a prerequisite for basic services. The goal is the elimination of anonymity: the state ensures that a citizen cannot walk down a street or access the internet without being digitally identified.

The Spiral of Silence

A palpable shift in public behavior occurs without new laws being passed. People begin scrubbing their social media history, using encrypted apps for mundane chats, or speaking in coded language. This chilling effect signals that the population has internalized the surveillance. They are self-censoring because they assume the system is always watching and recording.

CITIZEN COUNTERMEASURES

Keeping Secrets Local

To defeat the "god view," resistance organizations often structure themselves into isolated cells. Information is shared strictly on a need-to-know basis. In this model, if one activist's device is infected with spyware, the damage is contained to their immediate contact list rather than exposing the entire organization. Decentralization removes the single point of failure that the panopticon seeks to exploit.

EAT AFTER READING

Deleting the Trail

Resilient networks operate on the assumption that all standard telecommunications (SMS, unencrypted calls) are compromised. Consequently, communication shifts to open-source, end-to-end encrypted tools that function outside the state's immediate reach. Crucially, the use of "disappearing messages" ensures data self-destructs. This minimizes risk, ensuring that if a device is seized by authorities, there is no historical data available to exploit.

Going Off the Grid

A return to low-tech tradecraft protects high-stakes planning. Critical meetings occur in person, outdoors, and strictly without mobile devices (which are left at home rather than merely turned off). Sensitive information travels via handwritten notes that are read and immediately burned, creating an "air gap" that no spyware can bridge.

WHERE DID MY BEDDING GO?
I SAW THE GOATS TAKE IT.

Scapegoating

DEFINITION

Scapegoating is the authoritarian tactic of exploiting an "other" to absorb public anger and deflect blame from those in power. When some crisis threatens legitimacy—or when a leader simply needs a convenient enemy to rally support—the regime redraws the social map into a simple "us versus them." A vulnerable group is singled out and blamed for the nation's decline. By converting complex problems into a human enemy, the leader unifies supporters through shared resentment and fear. The tactic relieves pressure on the regime and normalizes repression as collective self-defense. Once established, the scapegoat becomes a reusable political asset, activated whenever accountability looms.

EXAMPLE

A regime facing stagnation and corruption launches a campaign to "defend traditional values." State media begin portraying LGBTQ+ people as threats to children and families. Laws restrict public expression and ban LGBTQ+ advocacy. Officials insist the crackdown is not persecution, but protection. Protesters and journalists who object are accused of promoting immorality. As economic grievances mount, public attention is redirected toward policing identity and behavior rather than questioning leadership failures. The targeted community absorbs social anger, while the regime presents itself as the last line of defense between order and collapse.

TELLTALE SIGNS OF SCAPEGOATING

Blaming Small Groups for Big Problems

A leader causally links complex national issues to the specific actions or existence of a minority group. This narrative simplifies policy failures into a moral conflict, suggesting that the nation's "purification" or the group's removal is the only solution. By personifying abstract problems, the regime provides a visible target for public frustration, shielding leadership from accountability.

Creating a Fake Moral Crisis

The regime amplifies isolated incidents or supposed "threats" to suggest a widespread cultural or security crisis. This tactic often targets a group's lifestyle or values, representing them as an imminent threat to the "silent majority." This orchestrated urgency justifies the suspension of normal legal protections, presenting state-led repression as a necessary act of collective self-defense.

Calling Opponents Foreign Tools

Leaders often claim the targeted group is a "fifth column" secretly operating on behalf of hostile foreign powers or shadowy elites. This dual-threat narrative suggests the group is both culturally alien and a tool of national subversion. By branding dissenters or minorities as foreign assets, the leader delegitimizes their grievances and justifies harsh surveillance as a matter of national security.

CITIZEN COUNTERMEASURES

Proving We Are Alike

Scapegoating works by making a targeted group feel alien to their neighbors. The antidote is radical ordinariness. Sharing mundane, relatable narratives about the marginalized group through decentralized social media or community bulletins disrupts the psychological process of dehumanization before it hardens into public consent. When neighbors recognize themselves in the targeted group, the regime loses the social permission it needs to act.

Pointing Back at the Top

Simple infographics and community workshops can map current hardships directly to specific government policy failures, connecting inflation, corruption, and dysfunction to the leadership decisions that produced them. This breaks the diversionary tactic at its root, ensuring that public frustration finds its way to the source of the problem rather than the state-sponsored scapegoat.

Wearing the Target's Sign

Visible, collective acts of solidarity translate changed minds into a political problem for the regime. When a broad cross-section of the public physically adopts the symbols of a targeted group, it creates a normalization problem for enforcers and renders the scapegoat label socially impotent. The regime is forced into an impossible choice: abandon the narrative or launch an unpopular crackdown on the general population.

STAGE IV

The Theater of Democracy

Having seized the machinery of state, the *Tyrannus Rex* now begins to entrench and metastasize through the host system. Paradoxically, as its grip tightens, the creature learns that camouflage is as effective as terror. Modern authoritarianism does not abolish democratic institutions; it occupies them like a hermit crab. This stage explores the "zombie democracy," a system of hollow governing structures designed to simulate self-rule. Here, the law is twisted to shield the regime or ignored entirely when inconvenient, as there is no higher power to hold the leader to account. Combined with the empty rituals of voting without the possibility of real choice, the predator operates within a facade of choreographed legitimacy. To resist, we must distinguish the ritual from the reality. Drawing from the inventory of performative governance, we isolate ten distinct illusions to decode the stagecraft. We audit the capture. We expose the ruse. We tear down the curtains to end the charade.

IN THIS STAGE

Constitutional Vandalism • Controlled Opposition • Crony Capitalism
Faux Elections • Institutional Capture • Lawfare
Performative Leadership • Salami Tactics • Self-Coup • State of Exception

THE five COMMANDMENTS
Four Legs Good, Two Legs Better
NO ANIMAL SHALL SLEEP IN A BED with sheets.
NO ANIMAL SHALL DRINK ALCOHOL to excess.
NO ANIMAL SHALL KILL ANY OTHER ANIMAL without cause.
ALL ANIMALS ARE EQUAL but some are more equal than others.
DID WE VOTE ON THESE CHANGES?
NO VOTE REQUIRED. THESE ARE CLARIFICATIONS.

Constitutional Vandalism

DEFINITION

Constitutional Vandalism is the exploitation of democratic norms and unwritten rules under the cover of legality. Unlike overt coups or illegal power grabs, this tactic targets conventions that make constitutional systems function in practice: restraint, good faith, and respect for independent institutions. Tyrants often use legal loopholes to shut down or suspend legislatures at convenient moments, often to avoid votes or investigations. They lean on technicalities to delay accountability, intimidate courts without formally abolishing them, and turn neutral public institutions into partisan tools by installing loyalists in oversight roles. Each action is technically permissible, yet corrosive. Used strategically, constitutional vandalism consolidates power and reduces accountability while preserving plausible deniability. Though rarely criminal, it represents a profound breach of democratic trust.

THAT DOESN'T SEEM RIGHT.

EXAMPLE

A legislature begins moving toward a vote that would force the public release of damaging files tied to the regime. The initiative has rare bipartisan momentum and threatens to expose networks of influence that reach into the ruling party itself. Days before the vote can be scheduled, the head of the legislative body abruptly adjourns the chamber for a prolonged recess. The move is formally legal. No rules are broken. Yet the timing is decisive. Committees dissolve, motions expire, and public attention drifts. By the time the legislature reconvenes, the coalition has fractured and the moment has passed. Accountability has been avoided without a single law being violated.

TELLTALE SIGNS OF CONSTITUTIONAL VANDALISM

Exploiting Procedural Technicalities for Delay

The regime uses obscure parliamentary rules or legal loopholes to freeze legislative action exactly when accountability is imminent. By abruptly adjourning sessions or "proroguing" parliament during investigations, leaders stop democratic processes without breaking the law. These actions are technically legal but serve only to protect the executive from oversight, effectively turning the rulebook into a weapon against the spirit of the law.

Filling Independent Oversight with Loyalists

Authorities install partisan allies into non-political roles designed for neutral oversight, such as ethics committees, auditors, or election boards. While these appointments follow formal procedures, the new officials prioritize protecting the leader over performing their constitutional duties. This takeover of institutions ensures that even if a scandal is uncovered, the "independent" body responsible for investigating it will find no wrongdoing.

Breaking Norms Under the Cover of Legality

Leaders ignore long-standing democratic traditions like sharing information with the opposition or respecting judicial independence, while maintaining they are simply "following the letter of the law." By pushing executive power to its absolute legal limit without regard for the consequences to the system, they erode the trust needed for a democracy to function. This vandalism creates a system where power is exercised without the restraint that usually keeps it in check.

CITIZEN COUNTERMEASURES

Forcing Professional Consequences

Digital campaigns that target the professional organizations, universities, or social clubs of the officials involved can create a "professional tax" for their behavior. By tagging an official's law school or a board they sit on in a factual post about their role in procedural abuse, citizens trigger institutional pressure. This forces the official to defend their actions to their peers and mentors, rather than just their political base, making the cost of their "vandalism" feel personal and permanent.

Finding Legal Counter-Moves

Utilizing digital platforms to organize pro-bono legal experts and students helps identify obscure regulations or local laws that can compel stalled institutions to function. By finding specific legal mechanisms to force a legislature to reconvene or a committee to release files, citizens use the regime's obsession with "legality" against it. This proactive maneuvering turns the state's loophole strategy into a trap, creating friction that prevents the seamless consolidation of power.

Pressuring Local Officials

Coordinating high-volume, direct outreach to the specific officials facilitating procedural delays increases the personal cost of their obstruction. By engaging these figures through persistent correspondence and peaceful presence at their local offices, citizens remove the "clerical" anonymity of their actions. This tactic forces officials to choose between their loyalty to the executive and their continued social standing within their home communities.

FARM LEADERSHIP
ELECTION
ANIMALIST PARTY
REFORM PARTY
STABILITY PARTY
NAPOLEON
WHO DID I APPROVE AS THE REFORM CANDIDATE?

Controlled Opposition

DEFINITION

Controlled Opposition is the authoritarian tactic of neutralizing resistance by supporting fake rivals. Rather than banning opposition outright, the regime curates it. Approved parties and candidates are allowed to exist so long as they pose no genuine threat to power. They absorb public frustration, split the dissenting vote, and create the illusion of choice. Debates are staged and criticism is voiced, but always within boundaries set by the state. By managing opposition rather than eliminating it, the regime ensures that no matter who the citizen votes for, the outcome was never really in question.

EXAMPLE

A dominant ruling party permits several opposition parties to operate legally. Some are staffed by loyal insiders; others are quietly pressured into compliance through legal threats or kompromat. During elections, these parties campaign loudly against one another while avoiding direct challenges to the leader or core institutions. State media highlight their disagreements, describing the nation's politics as vibrant and competitive. Meanwhile, genuine opposition figures are disqualified and even jailed. Protest energy is diverted into sanctioned channels that cannot win. When public anger rises, the controlled opposition gains seats, not power, relieving public pressure without changing policy. The system appears democratic, but the outcomes remain fixed.

TELLTALE SIGNS OF CONTROLLED OPPOSITION

Selective State Tolerance

Authorities allow specific “rival” parties to hold rallies and access state media while aggressively suppressing others. If a dissident group is permitted to air grievances without facing arrests or censorship while genuine grassroots movements are criminalized, they are likely functioning as a release valve for public anger. This curated tolerance ensures that dissent remains visible and harmless to the regime’s core interests.

Strategic Policy Avoidance

Approved opposition figures focus their criticism on secondary issues or “culture war” debates rather than challenging the leader’s authority or signature policies. These actors play the role of the “loud critic” but consistently vote with the regime on essential legislation. This strategic avoidance ensures the spectacle of debate continues without ever threatening the regime’s grip on power.

Fragmentation of Dissent

The regime quietly funds multiple, small opposition parties that spend more energy attacking each other than the ruling power. By offering a crowded and chaotic political field, the state ensures that the anti-incumbent vote is split into ineffective fragments. This engineered infighting makes a unified front impossible, allowing the regime to maintain a majority while appearing to be just one of many competing interests.

CITIZEN COUNTERMEASURES

Joining Forces Outside the System

Establishing direct alliances between diverse grassroots groups such as labor unions, student organizations, and local neighborhood councils bypasses state-sanctioned political channels. By forming a unified front outside the official party system, citizens ensure that their collective demands are not filtered or diluted by approved "opposition" leaders. This horizontal coordination prevents the regime from splitting the movement and forces a genuine challenge to the ruling power.

Fact-Checking Opposition Claims

Requiring all groups claiming to represent the opposition to sign public pledges regarding funding sources and voting records exposes state-co-opted actors. Small community groups can use digital tools to track whether a "rival" candidate consistently aligns with the regime on critical issues or receives suspicious financial support. Publicly documenting these inconsistencies creates a litmus test for legitimacy, helping the public distinguish between genuine dissent and staged performance.

Refusing to Play Along

Coordinating a mass refusal to participate in "fixed" political rituals denies the regime the legitimacy it seeks. When citizens collectively ignore approved opposition channels, they collapse the theater of fake pluralism. This withdrawal of participation signals that the official "opposition" has no popular mandate, rendering the state's containment strategy ineffective.

PUBLIC-PRIVATE PARTNERSHIP
MY SONS EARNED THIS OPPORTUNITY.
FIREWOOD
EXCLUSIVE SELLER
BRICKS
EXCLUSIVE SELLER

Crony Capitalism

DEFINITION

Crony Capitalism is a rigged economic system where success is determined by relationships with government officials rather than by free-market forces. State resources, monopolies, lucrative contracts, and favorable regulations are selectively granted to a narrow inner circle of family members and political allies. In exchange, these "cronies" provide the regime with funding and media support. When loyal firms fail, the government absorbs their losses while their profits remain private, shielding the inner circle from accountability and binding them to the regime through shared complicity. The result is less a national economy and more a protection racket with a central bank.

EXAMPLE

A leader divides the national economy into fiefdoms—handing control of the energy sector to a brother, the construction industry to a childhood friend, and the media to a loyal donor. These "business leaders" do not need to be competent, just compliant. State-owned banks are ordered to issue massive loans to these favored firms without due diligence, and their debts are eventually socialized onto the public when the projects fail. Meanwhile, legitimate competitors are strangled by selective regulation, where tax audits and safety inspections are used to bankrupt anyone outside the circle.

HOW DID THEY "EARN" THAT?

TELLTALE SIGNS OF CRONY CAPITALISM

The Instant Oligarch

Watch for the rapid accumulation of vast wealth by individuals with no track record of business innovation. When the leader's childhood friend, former driver, or distant cousin is suddenly appointed to head a state-owned enterprise or wins a monopoly on imports, merit has been replaced by access.

Selective Enforcement

Regulatory agencies display a distinct bias: independent or opposition-aligned businesses face relentless tax audits, surprise safety inspections, and bureaucratic gridlock. Meanwhile, regime-aligned competitors operate with impunity, ignoring labor and environmental laws.

The "No-Bid" Epidemic

The contracts are rigged before they are written. No-bid awards and auctions designed with impossible prerequisites ensure that major infrastructure projects and government spending reach only one destination: a handful of firms linked to the ruling elite. Costs balloon and quality suffers, yet the same contractors win every tender.

CITIZEN COUNTERMEASURES

Mapping the Theft

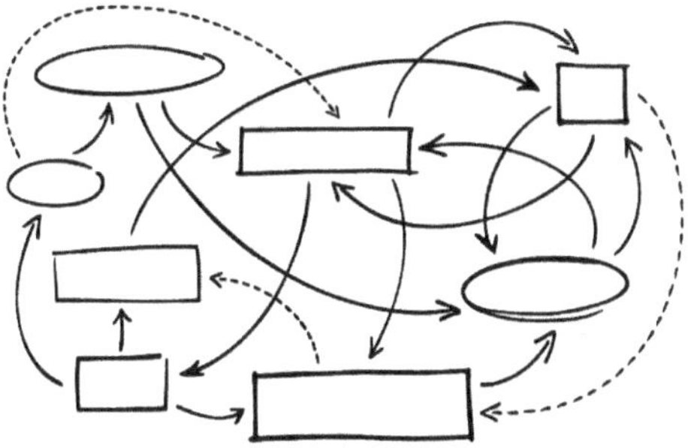

Civil society organizations leverage Open Source Intelligence (OSINT) to expose the hidden network of patronage. By cross-referencing public procurement data, luxury asset ownership, and offshore leaks, investigators visualize the web connecting politicians to their business proxies. When the precise mechanics of theft are revealed, the regime's narrative of national service is shattered by proof of its corruption.

Building a Leak Pipeline

The system relies on secrecy, so the resistance builds infrastructure to pierce it. Secure, anonymous reporting channels modeled on established whistleblower protection frameworks give conscience-driven civil servants and corporate insiders a legally defensible path to disclosure. When those inside the system know that safe, protected channels exist, the regime is forced to view its own bureaucracy with suspicion, paralyzing its ability to operate.

Squeezing the Crony's Wallet

Resistance movements identify and isolate the specific commercial entities funding the regime. Rather than broad, exhausting general strikes, consumers boycott the specific companies owned by cronies. This tactic squeezes the elite's revenue streams, turning their proximity to the dictator from a profitable asset into a financial liability, which creates internal friction within the ruling coalition.

VOTE
HERE
WINNER
Napoleon
VOTE SHARE
99%
BALLOT
BALLOT
TRASH

Faux Elections

DEFINITION

Faux Elections are staged electoral performances designed to mimic democracy while ensuring predetermined outcomes. Unlike traditional coups, which seize power openly, these rituals preserve the illusion of choice—it is democracy theater. The regime engages citizen participation through ballots and debates while aggressively controlling every variable behind the scenes. This involves disqualifying viable opposition, seizing control of election commissions, and saturating the media with state propaganda. The purpose is to portray an image of popular approval that discourages resistance and provides a veneer of legitimacy for domestic and international audiences. By rigging the mechanics of democracy, the leader invites the population to perform a script of consent that cruelly validates their own disenfranchisement.

EXAMPLE

An authoritarian permits an election to demonstrate their "faith" in the will of the people. Long before ballots are cast or viable opponents are barred, independent media are silenced, and election officials are handpicked from loyal ranks. On voting day, cameras capture long lines and waving flags, but behind the scenes, neutral monitors are excluded and ballot boxes are stuffed. Hours later, the leader claims a sweeping victory—98%, 87%, or another mathematically implausible number—declaring "the people have spoken." The next morning, state newspapers praise the unity of the nation and denounce skeptics as traitors. What looks like democracy is really just a coronation disguised as an election.

TELLTALE SIGNS OF FAUX ELECTIONS

Eliminated Opposition

Rival candidates are disqualified or disappeared long before a ballot is cast. Weaponized bureaucracy and lawfare do most of the work: endless paperwork requirements, spurious criminal charges, and administrative disqualifications leave only symbolic challengers on the field. There is no election. There is only a ceremony, and the guest of honor was chosen before the invitations went out.

Pre-Determined and Implausible Results

Vote counts are reported with impossible speed, non-existent variation, or mathematically suspect totals that defy polling data and logic. The electoral process exists to create the illusion of choice and produce pre-determined outcomes. The results prioritize neatness and uniformity over credible reflection of voter will.

Controlled Spectacle Followed by Rapid Consolidation

The regime stages mass patriotic rallies and choreographed media coverage, using performative transparency (like live broadcasts of ballot drops) to project legitimacy. Once victory is announced, it swiftly "closes the deal," purging remaining opponents and enacting pre-written, restrictive laws before domestic or international challenges can effectively mobilize.

CITIZEN COUNTERMEASURES

Conducting Parallel Vote Tabulations

When official counts are rigged, independent data becomes the primary form of resistance. Using Parallel Vote Tabulations (PVTs)—independent, statistically grounded "quick counts"—creates a verified baseline of results. Comparing these real numbers to regime totals rapidly exposes discrepancies before the official narrative hardens, creating actionable evidence that undermines the declared victor.

Campaigning to Expose the Fraud

Faux elections require faux opponents to maintain the illusion of choice. Utilizing the brief, legally-protected campaign window to publicly oppose the regime forces the autocrat into a strategic dilemma: either tolerate the dissent or openly silence it.
When the regime inevitably cracks down, the veneer of legitimacy dissolves, providing irrefutable proof of the fraud to a global audience.

Hitting the Streets En Masse

Mass mobilization after a stolen election is not merely protest. It is a public audit, conducted in bodies rather than ballots. Research consistently identifies 3.5% of the population as the threshold at which non-violent resistance becomes historically unstoppable. Organizing to reach this threshold does not merely protest the fraud.
It proves it.

THE FARM COURT
THAT IS UNLAWFUL.
I'VE EXPANDED THE COURT BY THREE SEATS.

Institutional Capture

DEFINITION

Institutional Capture is the conversion of neutral public institutions into instruments of partisan power. Rather than abolishing courts, regulatory agencies, intelligence services, or central banks, an aspiring autocrat quietly repurposes them by installing loyalists and rewriting internal rules to favor the ruling party. The goal is to eliminate any referees who can check their authority. Institutions that once constrained the regime are transformed into mechanisms that extend its reach. Institutional capture does not announce itself with a coup. It proceeds through appointments, budget maneuvers, procedural changes, and selective enforcement. By the time the public realizes the shift, the coup is already complete. No tanks were required. Only patience and the quiet rewriting of internal rules that nobody thought to watch.

EXAMPLE

An authoritarian frustrated by the independence of its central bank seeks to seize control. The leader begins by publicly attacking the institution, accusing it of sabotage whenever it issues inconvenient guidance. Loyal media echo the claim until the institution appears politically biased. The leader then nominates ideological allies or personal loyalists to key positions. Internal norms that protect independence are ignored or rewritten. Communications are increasingly filtered through political appointees. Over time, policy decisions that once rested on economic analysis shift toward serving the leader's short-term political needs. What was once a neutral institution becomes an extension of the ruling party, and the boundary between governance and personal rule dissolves.

TELLTALE SIGNS OF INSTITUTIONAL CAPTURE

Selective Weaponization of Oversight

Regulatory bodies suddenly lose their impartiality. Tax authorities, zoning boards, and ethics commissions launch aggressive investigations against opposition figures and independent media, while simultaneously ignoring flagrant violations by regime insiders. The laws are unchanged, but their enforcement becomes strictly one-sided.

Erosion of Civil Service Protections

The regime attacks the "tenure" or job security of career civil servants. By replacing permanent, professional staff with "at-will" political appointees, the leader removes the institutional memory and independence of the bureaucracy, ensuring that no one inside the agency is safe enough to say "no."

The Appointment of Unqualified Loyalists

The most visible sign is the placement of fierce partisans or personal friends into technical roles that traditionally require non-partisan expertise (e.g., a party propagandist appointed to lead the National Statistics Bureau or Department of Defense). This signals that the institution's priority has shifted from competence to compliance.

CITIZEN COUNTERMEASURES

Mobilizing Professional Guilds

Institutions rely on certified experts such as lawyers, doctors, and engineers who answer to external ethical codes. Mobilizing these professional associations (e.g., Bar Associations or Medical Boards) to censure or decertify collaborators imposes a high professional cost on "loyalists." When a captured judge or doctor is stripped of their license by their peers, it delegitimizes their authority and deters others from serving the regime.

Establishing "Shadow" Institutions

When the state captures the "referees," civil society must replace them. Creating parallel, non-governmental bodies to perform the state's lost functions, such as independent climate monitoring, pandemic tracking, or citizen-led electoral audits, denies the regime its monopoly on facts. These "shadow institutions" provide the public and international community with the baseline reality that the captured state tries to hide.

Slowing the Gears from Inside

Captured institutions still rely on bureaucracy, which is naturally slow. Honest civil servants remaining inside can exploit this inertia through "malicious compliance": following every minor regulation to the letter or "slow walking" procedures to slow down unethical orders. By demanding written instructions for every irregular request and burying political repression in mountains of procedural red tape, insiders can grind the machinery of capture to a halt without technically disobeying.

FRESH CARROTS FOR SAL
INSPECTED
C+
CITATION
VIOLATION
SUBPOENA
FINE
WE BELIEVE IN FREE AND FAIR ELECTIONS
ROUTINE INSPECTION.
YOU WERE HERE YESTERDAY.
REGISTER TO VOTE
D
VIOLATION
INSPECTE
C
VOTE

Lawfare

DEFINITION

Lawfare is the strategic abuse of legal systems to harass and incapacitate political opponents. The tactic weaponizes courts, prosecutors, regulatory agencies, and investigative bodies to persecute adversaries. Securing a conviction is seen as optional, as the primary objective is to make the process itself the punishment. By wielding the limitless resources of the state, the regime initiates a "slow-motion" campaign to inflict permanent reputational harm and drain the target's financial reserves. The victim is typically not imprisoned. They are simply made too exhausted, too broke, and too legally encumbered to remain a threat. All of it conducted, officially, in the name of justice.

EXAMPLE

A vocal critic refuses to endorse the ruling party. Within weeks, prosecutors open investigations into paperwork errors, decades-old business transactions, and tax filings that would never warrant a second glance under normal circumstances. Multiple agencies file overlapping charges, each requiring legal fees the target can barely afford. Hearings are delayed and rescheduled without explanation. Travel bans are imposed "pending review," effectively trapping the critic in place. State media report the allegations as settled fact, poisoning the public record before a single charge is proven. The damage is not delivered in a courtroom. It is delivered in the accumulated weight of legal fees and a reputation that can never be fully restored.

TELLTALE SIGNS OF LAWFARE

Selective Enforcement and Asymmetrical Scrutiny

The hallmark of lawfare is the asymmetrical application of legal scrutiny based on political loyalty. Loyalists committing serious offenses face no scrutiny, yet opponents are aggressively pursued for minor infractions and technicalities. The law is not enforced. It is weaponized.

Coordinated Use of State and Media Apparatus

Lawfare is a synchronized campaign involving both state agencies and media. Regulators launch surprise audits simultaneously with the announcement of investigations, amplifying the sense of guilt. State-controlled media report on the unproven allegations as established fact, ignoring legal rebuttals. This "trial by media" inflicts maximum reputational damage before conviction, confirming that the objective is public coercion and political destruction, not judicial fairness.

Process as Punishment

The legal process itself is the weapon, aimed at attrition rather than quick justice. The target is overwhelmed by multiple, overlapping charges, perpetual delays, and procedural hurdles. Indictments and cases that are tossed out by the courts are refiled without shame. The objective is to exhaust the opponent's finances, time, and reputation, using limitless state resources to grind down the opposition until they are neutralized and made to suffer.

CITIZEN COUNTERMEASURES

Funding the Defense

Lawfare relies heavily on financial attrition to silence targets. Establishing a visible defense fund to cover legal fees and investigations is a proven countermeasure. Pooling resources from outside the regime's reach guarantees the defense remains funded. This mitigates the "process as punishment" tactic and demonstrates widespread political solidarity, ensuring the target cannot be bankrupted into silence.

Winning the Public Trial First

Regimes use "trial by media" to convict the accused before court proceedings begin. Preempting this by immediately publishing all evidence through independent channels is critical. Exposing the political motivations behind charges shifts public perception from guilt to persecution. This transparency undermines the regime's narrative before it solidifies, turning the courtroom into a platform for exposing the state.

Naming the Judges and Prosecutors

Prosecutors and judges enable lawfare when they face no personal cost. Documenting and publicizing the professional ties and actions of these officials creates essential accountability. Imposing a reputational cost makes future advancement or international legitimacy difficult for these enablers. This increases the friction within the judicial system and creates a powerful disincentive for participating in political repression.

JUSTICE PETUNIA
weaponizes the legal system

LEADERSHIP AUDITIONS
HE'S GOT THE RIGHT LOOK.
SMILE

Performative Leadership

DEFINITION

Performative Leadership is the authoritarian habit of staffing government with figures chosen for how they appear and perform on camera. Competence is treated as secondary, or even threatening. Officials are selected the way props are selected: for how they look, how many followers they bring, and how little they are likely to think for themselves. Policy success is measured by ratings and favorable media cycles rather than results. Institutions are hollowed out as complex policy is replaced by slogans, viral clips, and ritualized displays of dominance. Governing requires expertise. Entertaining requires only attention. The authoritarian has always known which is easier to fake.

EXAMPLE

A leader fills senior government posts with television personalities, podcasters, and loyal media figures. These appointees deliver rehearsed talking points and attack critics, but lack the expertise to manage crises or complex systems. When one contradicts the leader or mishandles an emergency, they are quietly removed and replaced with another familiar face from the media ecosystem. Because the replacements look and sound interchangeable, the change barely registers with the public. This disposability is intentional. Unlike career professionals, who accumulate institutional knowledge and independent authority, talking heads are easy to swap out and discard. Continuity of the spectacle matters more than continuity of governance.

TELLTALE SIGNS OF PERFORMATIVE LEADERSHIP

Prioritizing Media Fluency Over Expertise
Appointments are consistently given to individuals with high-profile backgrounds in entertainment or media rather than relevant technical or administrative fields. The regime favors "screen-ready" candidates who can read from scripts and deflect criticism. This results in a leadership class that excels at projecting authority while possessing little to no experience managing the actual functions of the agencies they lead.

Measuring Success Through Engagement
Policy effectiveness is evaluated by public sentiment, viewership numbers, or social media virality rather than tangible social or economic indicators. Officials prioritize actions that generate immediate "optics" wins or aggressive soundbites, even if those actions are legally or logistically unsound. In this environment, a successful press conference is treated as more significant than a successful policy implementation, turning governance into a ratings-driven endeavor.

HE'S EASY ENOUGH TO SWAP OUT.

Interchangeable and Disposable Staff
Senior officials are treated as temporary cast members who can be dismissed and replaced without disrupting the regime's core narrative. Because these figures lack independent authority or institutional roots, their removal does not signal a change in policy, but rather a "refresh" of the spectacle. This disposability ensures that no subordinate gains enough popularity or expertise to challenge the leader, keeping the focus entirely on the head of state.

CITIZEN COUNTERMEASURES

Keeping the Failures on File

Documenting the specific failures of performative appointees through the collection of administrative data and public service outcomes exposes the gap between optics and reality. Small groups utilize digital spreadsheets to track unfulfilled promises, budget mismanagement, and service degradations. By presenting these objective failures in simple, shareable formats, citizens erode the "competence" narrative of the media-ready officials and force a focus on measurable governance.

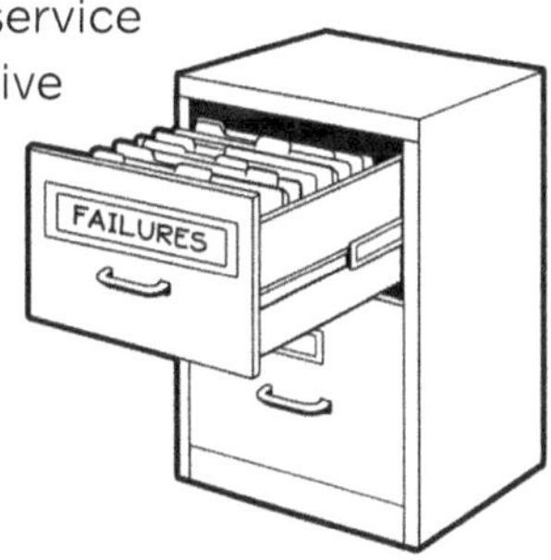

Demanding Technical Accountability

Filing frequent, targeted public information requests for the specific credentials and daily schedules of performative appointees highlights their lack of technical involvement. By asking for internal memos, policy drafts, and meeting minutes, citizens demonstrate that these figures are disconnected from actual decision-making processes. This administrative pressure reveals the leaderless nature of the institution, proving the appointee is a narrative placeholder rather than a functioning administrator.

Mocking Strategic Spectacle

Utilizing humor and satire to deconstruct highly produced state media reduces the psychological impact of the leader's projected dominance. When community groups create parody content or "fact-check" viral clips in real-time, they break the immersion of the political theater. This mechanism lowers the status of performative leaders, transforming an intended display of power into an object of public ridicule, which diminishes their charismatic authority.

FARM COMMITTEES
THE CENTRAL COMMITTEE
THERE USED TO BE SO MANY MORE. WE'D ARGUE. WE'D TALK.

Salami Tactics

DEFINITION

Salami Tactics are the step-by-step dismantling of the opposition through a series of actions that seem minor in isolation but are devastating in their cumulative effect. Rather than dismantling institutions all at once, the authoritarian slices away at them piece by piece, capturing one ministry, censoring one paper, outlawing one party wing at a time. Each cut is presented as temporary or necessary for "security," so the public tolerates it. By the time the greater pattern becomes unmistakable, the opposition has already been surrounded. The tactic succeeds because each slice, taken alone, never quite justifies the alarm. By the time the pattern is undeniable, the salami is gone.

EXAMPLE

A governing party enters a fragile coalition following national upheaval. It requests control of the Interior Ministry, arguing that public order must be restored. Soon after, it pressures broadcasters to silence "harmful" voices and quietly purges civil servants who are deemed insufficiently loyal. Rival factions within the opposition are courted, isolated, or outlawed in turn, each justified as a narrow measure against "extremism." Step by step, the space for dissent contracts. Newspapers close, parties fracture, elections become symbolic. No single move looks like a takeover, yet the cumulative effect is decisive. By the time citizens recognize the transformation, the salami has been sliced to the rind.

TELLTALE SIGNS OF SALAMI TACTICS

Focus on Capturing Critical Control Nodes Incrementally

The primary sign is a series of seemingly unrelated moves focused on capturing nodes essential for control, rather than broad, sweeping changes. The authoritarian targets the Interior Ministry (security), state broadcasters (information), and electoral bodies (power) one by one. Each "slice" is limited, but the cumulative effect ensures the regime gains unchallengeable control over the means of coercion, communication, and election certification.

Asymmetrical Treatment of Opposition Factions

The tactic relies on dividing the opposition before destroying it. The authoritarian exhibits an asymmetrical approach to rival factions, initially courting, accommodating, or leaving untouched the moderate wing while focusing on isolating the extremist or most vocal wing. This divides the opposition's resources and ensures they cannot present a unified front until all factions have been progressively sliced away.

Selling Each Action as Limited, Necessary, or Temporary

Each incremental step is justified using benign language to minimize public resistance. The authoritarian proclaims the capture of an institution as a "necessary security measure," and the purging of civil servants as "anti-corruption reform." This intentional downplaying of the cumulative threat leads the public and opposition to tolerate moves that appear too small to resist.

CITIZEN COUNTERMEASURES

Describing the "Big Picture"
Connecting seemingly disparate and minor slices into a single overarching narrative is critical. Naming this pattern as a "salami tactic" or "incremental coup" demonstrates that the cumulative effect is a full-scale assault on democracy. This breaks the illusion of smallness and compels the public to recognize the true scale of the threat before it is too late.

Drawing a Red Line
Establishing a broad coalition to define a non-negotiable "Red Line" is a proven deterrent. This body announces a specific threshold that, if crossed, triggers a predetermined and coordinated response. This pre-commitment forces opposition unity and creates a massive, visible cost for the next slice, often causing the regime to recalculate or pause its advance.

DO NOT CROSS DO NOT CROSS DO NOT CROSS DO NOT CROSS

Shaming the Mid-Level Enablers
Applying focused pressure on local and mid-level officials who implement unconstitutional orders can be a powerful lever. Publicizing the specific names and actions of these enablers creates immediate personal accountability. This imposes a reputational cost that increases internal friction, making it significantly harder for the regime to find willing hands to execute the next step.

COMPLICIT OFFICIALS

hold them accountable

EXECUTIVE DECREE

FROM THIS MOMENT FORWARD, I WILL GOVERN DIRECTLY.

Self-Coup

DEFINITION

A Self-Coup occurs when a democratically elected leader uses the authority of their office to dismantle the very institutions that elected them. Instead of seizing power from the outside, the leader consolidates it from within, claiming that parliament, the courts, or other checks on executive authority are obstructing the "will of the people." Under the guise of restoring order or ending corruption, the leader suspends constitutional limits and concentrates power in the executive branch. The process is presented as legal and necessary, even patriotic. Emergency decrees become routine and legislatures are sidelined or dissolved. What begins as a temporary expansion of authority hardens into permanent rule.

SOMEONE HAS TO RUN THINGS.

EXAMPLE

A leader facing political gridlock declares that existing institutions have become corrupt. With military or security forces standing by, they announce the dissolution of the legislature and the suspension of judicial oversight. State media present the move as a bold correction, insisting that decisive authority is needed to "restore stability" and "protect the nation from internal sabotage." Opposition leaders are arrested or forced into hiding, while new loyalist bodies are created to replace the dismantled institutions. The constitution remains in theory, but power now flows from a single office backed by force. What began as an elected presidency ends as an autocratic regime.

Dismantling Competing Institutions

The leader suspends or dissolves independent checks on executive power. This is a rapid strike to dismiss or pack the Supreme or Constitutional Court, dissolve the legislature or parliament, and place key independent bodies under executive control. This maneuver leaves the leader with unchecked power, often announced under the guise of removing "obstructions to the people's will."

Declaring the Action as Legal and Popular

The leader claims the unconstitutional move to be a necessary, legal, and patriotic defense against some crisis (e.g., security threat or institutional paralysis). This involves claiming pseudo-legal authority via loyalist decrees, while state media insist the decisive action is needed to "restore stability" and "protect the nation" from internal sabotage, giving the coup a veneer of democratic legitimacy.

Visible Support from State Security Forces

A self-coup requires the compliance of the state's coercive apparatus. A reliable sign is the visible presence and cooperation of military or internal security forces at the time of the announcement. Forces are immediately deployed to arrest opposition leaders and enforce the new decrees, confirming that the power now flows from a single executive office backed by guaranteed and immediate force.

CITIZEN COUNTERMEASURES

Blocking the Buildings

The first few hours and days are critical. Immediate and massive non-violent street protests that exceed the regime's capacity for arrest produce the best outcomes. The primary goal is not to fight the military but to physically deny the executive control over key institutions (e.g., surrounding the parliament, state media buildings, and courts) and to demonstrate that the supposed "will of the people" is opposed to the coup.

Shutting Down the Economy

Coordinated, high-impact economic shutdowns, primarily through a general strike organized across unions, major industries, and public transport, have proven effective. These aim to freeze the economy and render the state ungovernable within days. By threatening catastrophic economic instability, citizens impose a massive cost on both the regime and the business/security elite, often serving as the decisive factor that compels the military and business leaders to withdraw support.

Calling on the Soldier's Oath

Non-violent confrontation of security forces, demanding loyalty to the nation's foundational law (constitution, charter, etc.), is perilous but powerful. By personally appealing to soldiers' oaths and publicly documenting every order for unconstitutional violence, citizens apply pressure. This tactic is designed to break the chain of command and encourage defections, which is historically the most decisive factor in reversing a self-coup.

PUBLIC SAFETY EMERGENCY
FARM-WIDE CURFEW
7PM TO 9AM
REMAIN IN ASSIGNED AREAS
~~FOR 2 WEEKS~~
~~FOR 1 MONTH~~
~~FOR 3 MONTHS~~
UNTIL FURTHER NOTICE
NO POINT WAKING ANYONE AT SUNRISE. THEY CAN'T GO ANYWHERE.

State of Exception

DEFINITION

A State of Exception is the declaration of an emergency that allows an authoritarian leader to suspend constitutional protections while maintaining a facade of legal legitimacy. A pandemic, domestic unrest, a terrorist attack—any crisis will do. What begins as a temporary response is deliberately prolonged until emergency rule becomes the standard mode of governance. Civil liberties are restricted, legislatures are sidelined, and executive power is aggressively expanded through administrative decrees. The law remains in force in principle, but its protections are selectively switched off for political opponents. By ruling through exception, the leader converts extraordinary, time-limited powers into standard operating procedure, while insisting that every action they take is strictly lawful.

EXAMPLE

After what appears to be a domestic terrorist attack, the government declares a sweeping emergency. Civil liberties are suspended "temporarily" to restore order. Police are granted broad powers of arrest, homes are searched without warrants, and opposition newspapers are shut down for security reasons. Political rivals are detained as suspected accomplices. Soon after, the leader argues that emergency decrees are insufficient and demands new legal authority to govern without parliamentary approval. Legislators are pressured, intimidated, or excluded from the vote. The measure passes as a short-term necessity. In practice, it nullifies the legislature entirely. What began as an emergency response becomes a permanent transfer of power.

TELLTALE SIGNS OF STATE OF EXCEPTION

Creating a Permanent Crisis

The leader identifies a singular, catastrophic threat and uses it to justify the suspension of rights. A terrorist act, a pandemic, or an economic collapse each serve the purpose equally well. While the initial event may be real, the leader continuously redefines the "emergency" to ensure it never officially ends. This creates a psychological environment where the public accepts a new normal of total state control as the only alternative to chaos.

Shifting Lawmaking to Executive Decree

Legislative bodies are sidelined or dismissed under the pretense that traditional lawmaking is too slow to handle the current emergency. Instead, the leader begins governing through direct orders and administrative decrees that bypass public debate and judicial review. This concentrates all functional power in the executive office while leaving the shell of the constitution intact.

Suspending Rights with No Sunset Clause

Emergency powers are introduced without a clear, legally binding expiration date or measurable success criteria. If the regime refuses to define exactly when the emergency will end or what specific conditions must be met to restore civil liberties, the "exception" has become the rule. This lack of a sunset clause is a primary indicator that the leader intends to govern indefinitely without constitutional constraints.

CITIZEN COUNTERMEASURES

Keeping Power Local

Local officials can use municipal laws to refuse cooperation with federal emergency orders that overstep constitutional bounds. By passing ordinances that protect residents from unauthorized searches or arrests, cities create "legal islands" where the exception is ignored. This forces a direct conflict between levels of government, slowing the central leader's ability to enforce rules without local help.

Suing for Every Inch

Legal experts can launch constant challenges against specific emergency actions in lower courts. Even when high courts are pressured, individual cases regarding property or arrests can be won locally. These small victories create a "justice system shield," preventing power from concentrating in one office and forcing the regime to publicly justify its moves in a courtroom.

Exposing the Fake Security

Independent groups can publish data showing that "iron fist" emergency rules fail to improve safety and instead increase corruption. By highlighting how these policies lead to higher crime and administrative abuse, critics break the public's psychological support for the exception. When the majority realizes they are trading rights for false security, the leader loses their mandate.

STAGE V

The State of Terror

If the patterns in this section resonate with your reality, the diagnosis is grave. We have reached the terminal phase. Eventually, the pretense of law becomes a liability, and the mask falls away. In this final stage, the *Tyrannus Rex* is at its most dangerous, unburdened by the need for camouflage and driven by existential paranoia. It no longer seeks to persuade or deceive, but to dominate absolutely. The tools of the state are now turned inward: disappearances, extrajudicial detentions, and the systematic erasure of dissent. This is the endgame where the state exists solely to perpetuate the predator, and the citizen is reduced to a unit of production or a target of elimination. To resist here is to fight for survival. We must refuse to be broken. Drawing from the archives of repression, we isolate ten instruments of brutality to expose the machinery of dread. We map the network. We name the enforcers. We overcome the terror to survive the night.

IN THIS STAGE

FAIR FEED FOR ALL
FAIR FEED FOR ALL
FAIR FEED FOR ALL
FAIR FEED FOR
FAIR FEED FOR

Agents Provocateurs

DEFINITION

Agents Provocateurs are individuals covertly inserted into opposition movements to incite illegal acts that can be used to justify repression. They are state-sponsored antagonists. Their mission is to become indistinguishable from genuine protesters, then create the violence or chaos that justifies treating all protesters as criminals. When disorder erupts, the regime characterizes the crackdown that follows routine law enforcement. The tactic is particularly corrosive because it undermines trust. Movements begin to suspect their own members, fragmenting solidarity and paralyzing coordination. Over time, fear of infiltration becomes as damaging as infiltration itself, exhausting the opposition from within.

EXAMPLE

Citizens take to the streets as democracy itself is being dismantled. The demonstration remains peaceful, with organizers urging calm. Hours in, unfamiliar figures appear at the edges of the crowd. They blend in easily enough, but something is off. Their boots match. Their movements are coordinated. They communicate in ways that ordinary protesters do not. Then the windows start breaking. Projectiles fly. Police lines are rushed. State officials condemn the "riots," insisting the movement was never peaceful at all. Under the guise of restoring order, security forces sweep up both provocateurs and genuine protesters, though the former are quietly released while the latter face charges. The next day, public sympathy turns against the protesters, and the movement collapses.

TELLTALE SIGNS OF AGENTS PROVOCATEURS

The Escalation to Violence Without Strategy

The most consistent sign of a provocateur is the push for immediate, often senseless, violence that offers no strategic advantage to the movement. Genuine activists, even radical ones, usually debate tactics and worry about consequences. A provocateur skips the debate. They will urge a peaceful crowd to "burn it down," "kill the cops," or "storm the building" right now.

Possession of Specialized Equipment or Knowledge

Provocateurs often arrive "too ready." While organic protesters might have improvised gear, provocateurs frequently appear with specialized, high-grade equipment, such as military-grade comms, matching boots, specific incendiary devices, or pallets of bricks conveniently placed in advance.

Immunity from Consequence

The ultimate tell occurs after the violence. A provocateur often commits the first illegal act (throwing the first bottle, breaking the first window) but is rarely the one arrested. Police lines will often miraculously open to let them pass, or they will be "detained" briefly and released without charge while those caught up in the chaos face felonies.

CITIZEN COUNTERMEASURES

Using the Sit-Down

When agitators begin throwing objects or attacking police, the surrounding crowd immediately sits on the ground. This visual separation leaves the provocateurs standing alone, denying them a human shield and making it impossible for the regime to claim the entire group is violent. The instigators are instantly isolated and exposed.

Filming the Instigators

Provocateurs operate best in the fog of the front line. The counter is turning cameras away from the police and directly onto the agitators. Narrating the disavowal live—"We do not know this person!"—while filming their face and identifying marks, such as tattoos, destroys their anonymity. This creates an evidentiary record that protects the group and forces the exposed agent to flee.

WE DO NOT KNOW THIS PERSON!

Deploying Peace Marshals

Movements must police themselves. Deploying "Peace Marshals" creates a buffer against contagion. When a provocateur incites violence, Marshals move between the instigator and the crowd, facing the peaceful group with their backs to the agitator. This physically screens the movement from the bad actor without restraining them, visibly signaling to cameras that the violence is an isolated act rejected by the group.

BARNYARD INTERNAL CONTROL ENFORCEMENT
BICE
COOPERATE, OR BE CORRALLED!
BICE
BICE
BICE
I'M SURE THEY DON'T MEAN ME.

Brownshirts

DEFINITION

Brownshirts are paramilitary groups organized or tolerated by an authoritarian regime to enforce ideological conformity and extend state power beyond legal limits. The term originates from the *Sturmabteilung* (SA), the Nazi Party's original paramilitary wing, whose brown-uniformed members used street violence to terrorize political rivals in Weimar Germany. Their purpose is not to reinforce local police or bolster national defense, but rather to be the unofficial enforcement arm of the regime. In modern form, "Brownshirts" need not wear uniforms or even be official: they may be "volunteer militias," "loyalist movements," or co-opted state-sanctioned enforcement agencies. What defines them is not appearance but function: they operate above the law and use fear and intimidation as their primary governing tool.

EXAMPLE

An authoritarian announces the formation of "citizen defense brigades" to help restore order amid unrest. The groups are granted vague authority and encouraged to act where police are "overstretched." Members patrol demonstrations, intimidate organizers, vandalize opposition offices, and forcibly remove journalists from public spaces. Law enforcement remains conspicuously passive, occasionally coordinating routes or sharing intelligence. When violence escalates, officials praise the brigades' patriotism and restraint while victims are blamed for provoking conflict. Over time, the militias receive funding, equipment, and official titles, folding them into the state's security architecture. They answer to one authority. Not the law. Not the constitution. The leader.

TELLTALE SIGNS OF BROWNSHIRTS

Public Justification with Plausible Deniability

The regime publicly defends the group's actions while denying their true purpose. The cover story adapts to the circumstance. Unofficial militias are disowned but celebrated as patriots. Co-opted state agencies are acknowledged, but their terror is branded as law enforcement. The script changes. The impunity does not.

Politicized Targets

The group's violence and intimidation are not random. They are aimed exclusively at the regime's ideological or political opponents. While they may selectively target "crime," their primary purpose is to harass protesters, vandalize opposition party offices, intimidate journalists, or terrorize minority groups that the regime has scapegoated.

Selective Impunity

When these "loyalist" groups commit conspicuous acts of assault, vandalism, or harassment, the official police are slow to respond. If arrests are made, charges are mysteriously dropped or sentences are exceptionally light. This demonstrates that the group is operating above the law, serving as an unofficial, parallel enforcement arm of the state.

CITIZEN COUNTERMEASURES

Naming the Faces

Authoritarian enforcers rely on anonymity and the "superior orders" defense to justify repression. Stripping away these shields is critical. Collecting names, photos, and ranks creates a permanent record for future legal proceedings. Reminding enforcers that international law rejects "just following orders" as a valid defense transforms their perceived impunity into long-term personal liability.

Pressuring the Courts

Systemic impunity thrives when local systems remain silent. Filing police reports for every abuse or criminal act forces the judicial infrastructure to respond. Demanding public condemnation from local officials creates a binary choice: enforce the law or expose complicity. This accumulation of administrative pressure increases the political friction of ignoring state-sponsored violence.

Standing Beside the Targets

Paramilitary terror relies on isolating targets to maximize fear. Mobilizing volunteers or international observers to physically accompany at-risk individuals counters this tactic. When witnesses stand beside the threatened, acts of intimidation become matters of public record rather than private trauma. This visible solidarity turns the regime's weapon of fear into a liability.

NO WATER FOR GOATS
WHY CAN'T WE HAVE WATER?
BECAUSE A FEW GOATS SPOKE UP.

Collective Punishment

DEFINITION

Collective Punishment is the practice of retaliating against the families and communities of dissidents for the actions or beliefs of one individual. Rather than targeting dissent directly, the regime weaponizes social bonds. By threatening spouses and children, the state ensures that resistance carries an unbearable moral cost: the reckless endangerment of innocents. This exploits the deepest human instinct to protect one's kin, making silence feel like an ethical obligation rather than a surrender. Over time, citizens stop policing the regime. They start policing each other. The result is a society where the state barely needs to enforce obedience because fear does it instead.

EXAMPLE

A regime identifies a citizen as a critic of the state. Instead of charging the individual alone, security forces detain parents, siblings, and sometimes neighbors and distant relatives. No hearings are held. Children are taken with adults, including those born after the alleged offense. Entire family lines are erased from public life and transported to labor camps. The accused may disappear, but the punishment endures across generations. Communities quickly learn the lesson: political conformity is a survival strategy. People police their own thoughts, friendships, and speech to protect those they love. Over time, citizens are conditioned to equate loyalty to the state with loyalty to their own family.

TELLTALE SIGNS OF COLLECTIVE PUNISHMENT

Linking Community Identity to Individual Acts

The state officially blames an entire group for the actions of a few individuals. Leaders use the "one of them" narrative to justify broad restrictions, claiming that the group's culture or ideology makes everyone within it complicit. This logic transforms a single crime into a community-wide offense, providing the regime with a pretext to punish thousands of innocent people simultaneously.

Withholding Basic Needs as Discipline

Authorities restrict access to water, electricity, food, or internet across specific neighborhoods or regions suspected of harboring dissent. This tactic is used to force the community to "police itself" by making the cost of non-compliance unbearable for everyone. When a leader uses survival as a bargaining chip, they are shifting from individual law enforcement to collective coercion.

Enforcing Guilt by Association

The regime introduces laws or policies that penalize the family members, business partners, or neighbors of suspected dissidents. By seizing the assets or restricting the travel of those related to an "enemy of the state," the leader turns personal relationships into a liability. This creates a powerful social deterrent, as individuals are forced to choose between their convictions and the safety of their loved ones.

CITIZEN COUNTERMEASURES

Running Mutual Aid

Establishing community-led systems for sharing food, water, and medicine ensures that the group can survive state-imposed shortages. By mapping local resources and creating decentralized distribution points, neighbors reduce the regime's ability to use "starvation tactics" as a tool for compliance.

Reporting the Harms

Recording the impact of broad sanctions on non-political entities like hospitals and schools exposes the regime's lack of precision. Sharing these findings through independent channels shifts the narrative from "targeted security" to "indiscriminate aggression." This evidence-based documentation attracts neutral observers to the resistance cause and raises the domestic and international reputational costs for the state's enforcers.

Withholding the Payments

Coordinating economic slowdowns in targeted regions, through work stoppages, market boycotts, and the withdrawal of discretionary spending from regime-aligned businesses, turns the state's punishment into a financial liability. When multiple communities withdraw economic participation simultaneously, the revenue consequences are difficult for the state to address through individual enforcement without escalating the very conflict it sought to suppress.

HAVE YOU SEEN GLADYS?
WHO'S GLADYS?
BERNICE
DAISY
BEGONIA
GLADYS

Enforced Disappearance

DEFINITION

Enforced Disappearance is the state's ultimate "stealth" weapon. Instead of making a public example of a dissident, the regime abducts them and removes them from all legal and public visibility. Some victims are murdered in secret and their bodies destroyed; others are kept alive in undisclosed detention sites, unseen by courts, families, or humanitarian monitors. In both cases, the state denies any knowledge of the person's whereabouts, erasing them from official existence. By reducing a human being to a missing-person statistic, the regime coldly exploits uncertainty. Families remain trapped between hope and grief, unable to mourn or mobilize. That unresolved limbo becomes a tool of social control, warning everyone that disappearance can strike without warning and leave no trace.

EXAMPLE

A dissident leaves work one evening and never arrives home. Witnesses note an unmarked car or a sudden street scuffle, but nothing is officially recorded. When the family contacts the police, they are told no arrest occurred. Hospitals have no entry. Courts have no case. The state neither confirms nor denies involvement, insisting the person must have fled or fabricated their own disappearance. Privately, the abductee is held in an undisclosed location, interrogated, and killed. Their body is buried anonymously, burned, or dumped where it will never be recovered. Weeks later, officials deflect inquiries by demanding proof of a crime. The family cycles between hope and despair. The uncertainty is the point: when no one knows who will vanish next, fear becomes a form of social control.

TELLTALE SIGNS OF ENFORCED DISAPPEARANCE

The Administrative Vacuum

When family or lawyers inquire at police stations or hospitals, they are met with a wall of "No Record." The state does not deny the person exists; they simply deny that the state has interacted with them. This creates a terrifying sense that the person has simply evaporated from the face of the earth.

The Erasure of a Paper Trail

In the hours following an abduction, the regime's digital units scrub the victim's social media, "expire" their passport in the system, and may even delete security camera footage from the area where they were last seen. The goal is to make it look as if the person chose to go into hiding or walked away from their life.

Strategic Rumors of Defection

To deflect international pressure, the regime's proxies spread rumors that the disappeared person was actually a double agent who fled to a rival country, or that they were involved in a sordid criminal underworld. This poisons the victim's reputation while they are unable to defend themselves, making the public less likely to demand their return.

CITIZEN COUNTERMEASURES

Filing Immediate Petitions

The most effective defense is speed. Within minutes of a suspected abduction, human rights networks must flood the state's legal system with habeas corpus petitions, which are legal demands to "produce the body." Even if the state ignores them, the massive paper trail makes it harder to claim later that the person was never in custody.

Showing the Empty Chair

If the regime tries to erase a person, the opposition must make their absence as visible as possible. Using an empty chair at conferences, posting daily "Day [X] since disappearance" counters, and carrying photos of the victim prevent the "ghosting" from working. It forces the world to look at the hole the regime has created.

5
DAYS SINCE
GLADYS
DISAPPEARED

Tracing the Digital Footprints

Modern disappearances are harder to hide because of the digital breadcrumb trail. Independent investigators use cell tower pings, flight manifests, and leaked hotel registries to reconstruct the abduction. Once the specific "snatch squad" is identified and named, the regime often locates the prisoner in a jail somewhere to avoid being linked to a murder.

STOP
STEALING
OUR
EGGS
MR. JONES SET THE FIRE. THE GUARD IS FOR YOUR SAFETY.
THEY'RE TRYING TO END OUR STRIKE.

False Flags

DEFINITION

A False Flag is a covert operation engineered to appear as though it was carried out by someone else, typically an enemy or domestic opponent. The goal is to invent justification for repression, retaliation, or war by staging an attack and assigning blame to the targeted group. False flags exploit a simple psychological leverage point: outrage comes faster than verification. Once the public believes an adversary has struck first, fear and anger create immediate permission for the leader to take extraordinary action. Modern false flags need not be elaborate. They may involve a staged sabotage, a fabricated terrorist plot, or a manipulated "intelligence leak" that labels opponents as violent threats. The specific operation is irrelevant. The story it enables is what matters.

EXAMPLE

An authoritarian faces opposition they cannot easily silence. At a politically useful moment, a bomb "discovered" near a government building or a violent incident at a protest is immediately attributed to the regime's critics. State media release statements and "evidence" within hours, long before any independent investigation could occur. Officials insist the threat is imminent and demand emergency powers to respond. Security forces raid opposition offices, arrests follow, and civil liberties tighten. The inconsistencies always emerge eventually: missing footage, implausible timelines, anonymous "confessions." But the false flag does not need to survive scrutiny. It only needs to survive long enough. The public has already absorbed the emotional impact, and the crackdown proceeds under the banner of self-defense.

TELLTALE SIGNS OF FALSE FLAGS

Legislative Velocity and Pre-Packaging

Genuine crises produce initial chaos and delay, whereas false flags often produce immediate, complex solutions. If a massive legislative package or detailed military invasion plan is presented within hours of the event, it indicates the agenda preceded the crisis. This "solution in search of a problem" suggests the event was engineered to catalyze a pre-existing objective that the public would otherwise reject.

Operational Mimicry and Concurrent Drills

Historically, state-sponsored attacks frequently coincide with security exercises mimicking the exact scenario. This synchronization provides logistical cover, allowing operatives to move equipment under the guise of training without raising alarm. It also paralyzes the initial response, as emergency personnel struggle to distinguish between the simulation and the live event, ensuring the attack achieves maximum psychological impact.

Forensic Anomalies and Narrative Rigidness

False flags often rely on "pristine evidence" found in impossible conditions to quickly identify a convenient culprit. Conversely, the physical mechanics of the event often contradict the official explanation. A rigid adherence to a scientifically impossible narrative, combined with the rapid destruction or sealing of physical evidence, is a primary indicator of fabrication.

CITIZEN COUNTERMEASURES

Pausing the Panic Laws

False flags exploit shock to bypass debate. The primary defense is demanding an immediate legislative "pause." Contacting representatives to oppose any bill introduced within 48 hours of a crisis halts the momentum. By representing delay as "prudence" rather than "weakness," the state is forced to justify new powers without the cover of adrenaline.

Saving the First Reports

Official narratives often require scrubbing conflicting early reports to ensure consistency. Immediacy is key: archive live footage, local news segments, and eyewitness posts before they are sanitized. Creating a distributed, redundant backup of the initial chaos prevents the regime from streamlining the story later. This "digital preservation" ensures that initial contradictions remain visible and undeniable.

Protecting the Whistleblowers

The weakest point in any false flag is the human chain required to execute it. Operations of this scale involve planners, operatives, and witnesses, and any one of them can talk. The countermeasure is creating conditions that make talking feel safe. Visible public support for whistleblowers lowers the social and professional cost of disclosure, signaling to conscientious insiders that integrity will be honored rather than punished.

I DON'T WANT TO LIE TO EVERYONE.
REMEMBER, THESE PHOTOS WILL RUIN YOU.

Kompromat

DEFINITION

Kompromat—a Russian term for "compromising material"—refers to information collected or fabricated to coerce, control, or destroy an individual's credibility. While the term originated in Soviet intelligence practice, the concept is universal to authoritarian systems. It transforms private life into a weapon and trust into liability. For an authoritarian, kompromat is not a tool of last resort, it is a governing philosophy. Friends and enemies alike are subject to surveillance and the quiet accumulation of damaging secrets. Loyalty is enforced through blackmail. Every alliance becomes conditional, every confidant a potential hostage. In this system, morality is irrelevant; only leverage matters.

EXAMPLE

An authoritarian gathers private information on both adversaries and allies, from financial irregularities and tax discrepancies to the details of personal affairs. At first, the material is only used defensively: to silence critics or derail investigations. Over time, kompromat becomes the regime's central nervous system. Cabinet ministers, judges, and business elites learn that their careers, and sometimes their freedom, depend on the leader's discretion. Those without compromising material are not trusted; the innocent are the most dangerous of all. When a defector flees or a critic speaks out, a dossier is leaked at once: photos, transcripts, confessions. The aim is to ostracize the individual and make them a terrifying example, ensuring that others who are compromised choose absolute obedience over dissent.

TELLTALE SIGNS OF KOMPROMAT

Sudden, Unexplained Capitulation

An outspoken judge, rival politician, or business leader abruptly reverses course. Yesterday's fierce critic becomes today's reluctant endorser, citing vague "personal reasons" that explain nothing and convince no one. The shift is too sudden and too complete to be genuine. The simplest explanation is coercion: someone found their file.

Precisely Timed Leaks

A damaging story never arrives randomly. It surfaces just before an election, during a key vote, or at the precise moment an opponent gains traction, because kompromat is not journalism. It is a weapon, and weapons are deployed when they are needed most.

"Anti-Corruption" Campaigns

The regime declares a crusade to "clean up corruption" or "restore integrity," but only the opposition is ever cleansed. Corrupt loyal insiders remain untouched. This is kompromat in institutional form: the use of state prosecutors, auditors, and intelligence agencies to manufacture scandal under the cover of law.

CITIZEN COUNTERMEASURES

Making the Method the Real Scandal

Kompromat relies on the public fixating on the content of a leak. The real questions are who obtained the material and why it was released at this precise moment. Turning attention to the regime's surveillance tactics drains the leak of its moral force, shifting the scandal from the target's privacy to the state's corruption.

WHO GOT THIS STUFF?

WHY ARE THEY RELEASING IT NOW?

Crowdsourcing Counter-Research

While regimes use state machinery to investigate opponents, citizens can leverage Open Source Intelligence (OSINT) to scrutinize the leadership. Examining financial records, contracts, and public disclosures of the inner circle creates an asymmetric cost. Publishing these findings ensures that every smear campaign launched by the state invites a reciprocal exposure of its own corruption.

De-Stigmatizing Human Flaws

Blackmail thrives on shame and the demand for moral purity. Refusing to treat private, non-criminal behavior as worthy of attention strips this tactic of its power. When citizens normalize imperfection and prioritize governance over gossip, the regime's stockpile of "compromising material" loses its market value. This resilience protects opponents from being silenced by trivial exposures.

BICE RELOCATION CENTER
IT'S PROBABLY FOR THE BEST.

Mass Detention

DEFINITION

Mass Detention is the use of the state's coercive power to confine large groups of people without due process. Unlike ordinary incarceration, it relies on broad classifications rather than proven crimes. Identity, ancestry, religion, political belief, or legal status becomes sufficient cause for confinement. The camps are often justified as temporary security measures during crises, but their real function is control. By removing entire populations from public life, the regime subdues perceived threats and normalizes collective punishment. Legal safeguards are suspended or reinterpreted, and administrative orders replace courts. Detention becomes the regime's clearest statement of principle. Rights are not guaranteed. They are granted, and what is granted can be revoked.

EXAMPLE

Following a national emergency, the government declares that a specific population poses an internal security risk. Without evidence of individual wrongdoing, thousands are ordered to leave their homes and report to holding centers. Families are given days to dispose of property and businesses at a loss. They are transported under guard to remote camps surrounded by fences and watchtowers. No charges are filed. No trials occur. Officials insist the policy is protective rather than punitive, and courts defer to executive authority. Over time, confinement becomes routine. The emergency passes. The camps do not. And when the detainees are finally released, they return to lives the state destroyed and a society that passively watched it happen.

TELLTALE SIGNS OF MASS DETENTION

Normalizing Administrative Orders

Authorities bypass the court system by using executive decrees or "emergency" administrative orders to authorize long-term confinement. These orders remove the right to a trial or a lawyer, leaving detainees in a legal vacuum where they cannot challenge their imprisonment. When a leader claims that "public safety" is too urgent for traditional due process, it signals the transition to mass detention.

Using Euphemistic Language for Camps

The regime rebrands detention facilities with non-threatening names like "relocation centers," "training camps," or "temporary shelters" to mask their punitive nature. By controlling the vocabulary, the leader minimizes public alarm and moral resistance. This "sanitized" language helps the majority ignore the reality of barbed wire and armed guards, spinning mass incarceration as a benevolent or necessary social service.

Criminalizing Identity

The state shifts from investigating individual acts to targeting entire categories of people based on race, religion, or political affiliation. Laws are rewritten to define mere membership in these groups as a threat to national security. This allows the regime to detain thousands without needing to prove specific crimes, replacing the legal standard of "guilt" with the political standard of "identity."

CITIZEN COUNTERMEASURES

Blocking the Permits

Municipal zoning laws and environmental regulations have historically proven effective at blocking or significantly delaying the construction of detention facilities. Communities organizing at the local level to oppose land-use permits for federal or state contractors turn a national directive into a prolonged local legal battle. Every permit appeal, environmental review, and zoning variance required is time the regime does not have and money it must publicly justify.

Opening Sanctuary Spaces

Religious institutions, community organizations, and legal advocates have historically created protective networks for those facing discriminatory enforcement. Establishing know-your-rights training, legal observer programs, and rapid legal response teams ensures that individuals facing administrative arrest have immediate access to counsel before and during any enforcement action.

Flooding the Legal System

Habeas corpus, the ancient right to demand that the state justify any detention before a court, is among the most durable tools available to civil society. When volunteer lawyers and families flood the courts together, the cumulative pressure transforms individual acts of legal resistance into a crisis the regime cannot easily absorb. Mass detention depends on administrative invisibility. Flooding the courts strips that invisibility away.

WELCOME
TO
ZONE 6
ROUTINE CHECK. JUST KEEPING THE ZONE SAFE.

Pacification

DEFINITION

Pacification is the use of military force against a civilian population to suppress dissent. The violence is real. Only the justification is fabricated. The terminology is deliberately adversarial: protests become "riots," neighborhoods become "zones," and citizens become "targets." The objective is to break the social will to resist through overwhelming force. By militarizing everyday governance, the regime normalizes the presence of troops in civilian life and collapses the distinction between war and policing. Curfews, checkpoints, mass detentions, and surveillance are justified as temporary necessities, yet they linger long after unrest subsides. Over time, citizens adapt to the armored vehicles and patrols, and emergency measures harden into permanent routine.

EXAMPLE

After a period of mass violence and political chaos, a new ruler promises stability and national renewal. Declaring disorder itself the enemy, the regime embeds the military deep into civilian governance. Soldiers oversee local administrations, campuses, unions, and newsrooms. Political parties are neutered, the press is tightly managed, and civic organizations are folded into state-approved bodies. Public dissent is treated as a relapse into chaos and met with swift, visible force. The regime may deliver roads, jobs, and consumer goods alongside the repression, but the bargain is never stated openly: accept the boot, receive the bread. The bargain holds as long as no one questions it. And the regime ensures no one questions it twice.

TELLTALE SIGNS OF PACIFICATION

Redefining Dissent as Criminal Disorder

The regime uses language to transform political protesters into "rioters," "looters," or "threats to public safety." By framing civic opposition as a purely criminal or chaotic security problem, the leader justifies using combat-level force against civilians. This tactic allows the state to ignore the root causes of unrest while portraying violent suppression as a necessary service for the law-abiding majority.

Trading Civil Rights for Material Stability

The leader offers a "bargain" where the public receives improved infrastructure, steady consumer goods, or lower crime in exchange for total political silence. Material comfort is used as a psychological anesthetic to make the loss of freedom feel tolerable or even beneficial. Pacification is succeeding when the population begins to value order more than the right to participate in their own government.

Embedding Soldiers in Civilian Offices

Military officers are appointed to lead traditionally non-military institutions, such as schools, labor unions, and local utility boards. This creeping militarization ensures that every level of daily life is monitored by the state's security apparatus. When the distinction between a soldier and a city administrator disappears, the regime effectively turns the entire country into a controlled military zone.

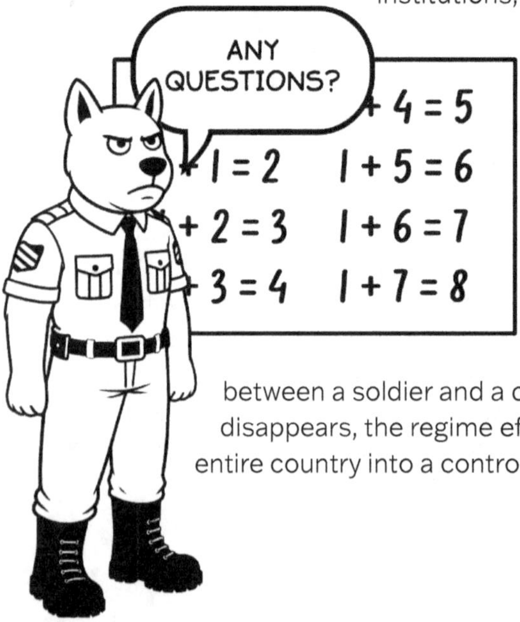

CITIZEN COUNTERMEASURES

Staying Non-Violent

Strictly refusing to engage in physical conflict or property damage prevents the state from justifying "pacification" tactics to the public. When a movement remains peaceful despite military provocation, the regime's use of force appears nakedly aggressive rather than a "restoration of order." This contrast breaks the state's narrative and can cause internal hesitation or defections within the security forces themselves.

Doing it Ourselves

Creating independent, community-run alternatives for education, news, and conflict resolution reduces reliance on militarized state offices. When citizens resolve their own disputes and share their own information, the regime's claim that military "administration" is necessary for stability collapses. These parallel structures serve as the foundation for a new society that exists right under the nose of the occupying forces.

Reclaiming Public Spaces

Using art, music, and community festivals to maintain a presence in "pacified" zones keeps the spirit of resistance alive without triggering a military response. These cultural occupations prove that the regime can control the streets but not the identity or morale of the people. By celebrating the community's values in public, citizens prevent the military from fully normalizing its presence in civilian life.

STANDARD PROCEDURE. ARREST ANYONE UNDER 10.
INNER CIRCLE
LOYALTY INDEX
NNIE — 16
TZ — 14
UE — 11
BAILEY — ~~10~~ 8
MAYBELL — 4
THISTLE — 1

Political Purges

DEFINITION

A Political Purge is the removal of individuals or factions from positions of power, typically under the guise of "anti-corruption" or "national security." The true purpose is simpler: eliminate rivals, silence dissent, and ensure that loyalty is total and unquestioned. The term borrows the language of cleansing, implying that what is being removed is diseased or corrupt. In practice, what is being removed is anyone capable of independent thought or collective action. Purges range from the theatrical to the bureaucratic, from mass arrests and televised show trials to forced resignations and quiet reassignments, but their dual function is constant. Those targeted are destroyed. Those who remain are traumatized into compliance. The purge does not need to touch everyone to control everyone.

EXAMPLE

An authoritarian, sensing disloyalty within the ranks, launches an "integrity campaign" to restore trust in the system. The purge begins quietly, with sudden firings of mid-level officials and the arrest of a few prominent critics under vague charges of corruption or conspiracy. Each week brings new accusations, new televised confessions, new "traitors" unmasked. Ministries compete to prove their devotion by purging their own members. Fear replaces initiative; silence becomes survival. What began as a purge of the disloyal ends as a purge of the capable. The leader stands alone at last, surrounded by people too frightened to tell the truth and too compromised to leave.

TELLTALE SIGNS OF POLITICAL PURGES

Selective Loyalty Tests

The purge begins with oaths, vetting procedures, or "anti-corruption" investigations that target not the incompetent, but the politically independent. Refusal to profess loyalty, sign public statements, or endorse the leader's specific line becomes the sole grounds for immediate dismissal or prosecution, prioritizing servility over competence.

Public Theater of Confession and Denunciation

Victims are often forced to "confess" fabricated crimes or moral failures in televised statements or internal meetings. These spectacles serve to validate the purge's righteousness, humiliate the accused, and teach the public that innocence offers no protection against the leader's will.

The Use of Vague Crimes

Targets are charged with vague crimes that can be stretched to fit any person or action. "Disloyalty," "extremism," and "being an enemy of the people" are not legal standards. They are blank warrants. The purpose is not to prove guilt, but to criminalize independence itself.

CITIZEN COUNTERMEASURES

Feeding the Families

Purges aim to destroy the social standing of the accused and their families. Countering this isolation by providing mutual aid or social validation to victims' families is a vital form of resistance. This support demonstrates that the regime's power is not absolute and prevents the intended psychological and economic annihilation of dissent.

Demanding the Charges

Demanding specific, concrete charges for every arrest is a primary defense against purges. These campaigns rely on vague crimes like "disloyalty." Insisting on provable violations under existing law exposes the political nature of the action. This pressure forces the regime to over-extend its authority, stripping the purge of its legal camouflage.

Refusing to Accuse

Purges depend on social fragmentation and forced denunciations to prove loyalty. Refusing to participate in this public theater of condemnation disrupts the chilling effect. Maintaining social ties and rejecting the presumption of guilt denies the purge its moral legitimacy. This quiet non-compliance preserves the essential bonds of civil society against decay.

THREE GOATS "FELL" FROM THAT WINDOW THIS WEEK.
ONLY CRITICS HAVE THAT PROBLEM.

Spectacle Executions

DEFINITION

Spectacle Executions are the targeted killing of high-profile dissidents using a distinctive method so that the regime's involvement is unmistakable. Unlike enforced disappearance, which hides the crime, a spectacle execution advertises it. The method is chosen for recognizability rather than efficiency: exotic toxins, radioactive substances, or carefully staged "accidents" that signal state capability. The regime creates a signature that broadcasts two messages at once: to the international community, a claim of plausible deniability; to domestic critics, a reminder that no distance or asylum can guarantee their safety. The execution functions as a deterrent by example, transforming a single death into a broadcast warning that punishment for dissent is inescapable.

EXAMPLE

A well-known dissident living in exile collapses after an ordinary encounter in a public space. Within days, physicians identify an extremely rare poison associated with state-controlled laboratories. The illness unfolds slowly and visibly, ensuring constant media attention. Medical updates replace press statements, and the victim's suffering becomes a global spectacle. Investigators trace the substance's origin, while the accused state dismisses the findings as fabricated or politically motivated. Diplomatic protests follow, but stall amid denials and procedural delays. For the intended audience, the lesson is clear. If a critic can be lethally targeted in a foreign land under international scrutiny, then silence, not distance, is the only safe option.

TELLTALE SIGNS OF SPECTACLE EXECUTIONS

The "Signature" Method

The death involves an unusual or poetic mechanism that clearly points back to the state's specialized capabilities. Whether it is a banned nerve agent, a specific radioactive poison, or the unlikely defenestration (falling from a window) of an otherwise healthy person, the method itself is the regime's branding.

Official Mockery and Victim Blaming

Immediately following the event, state-run media deny all involvement and proceeds to mock the victim. They may claim the victim was "unstable," a "traitor," or suggest they died during a salacious "personal matter." This prevents the victim from becoming a martyr by surrounding their death with a cloud of sordid rumors.

Consular or Sovereign Blind Spots

The attack often occurs in spaces where the regime holds a degree of legal or diplomatic immunity, such as an embassy, a consulate, or a foreign territory where the local government is either intimidated or bribed into looking the other way. This highlights the regime's ability to turn safe havens into kill zones.

CITIZEN COUNTERMEASURES

Giving Early Warnings

Intelligence agencies in democratic nations have a "Duty to Warn" individuals when they uncover credible threats. Publicly disclosing that a specific person is on a hit list can sometimes deter the attack by stripping away the element of surprise and making the regime's intent a matter of global record before they can act.

Freezing the Assets

Because the assassins and their handlers often rely on the global financial system to enjoy their wealth, targeted personal sanctions (freezing bank accounts and revoking visas) are highly effective. When the individual operatives and the oligarchs who fund them lose access to their foreign assets, the "cost" of the hit becomes higher than its political value.

Investigating the Squads

Regimes rely on the world "moving on" to the next news cycle. Independent investigative bodies (like Bellingcat or UN Special Rapporteurs) that use digital forensics and flight data to name the specific hit squad members break the regime's deniability. Making the operatives internationally wanted for the rest of their lives degrades the regime's ability to recruit future assassins.

Epilogue: The Extinction Event

We began this field guide with Benjamin Franklin's warning: "A republic, if you can keep it." At the start of the book, those words were merely an abstract historical caution. Now, you likely feel them in your bones. You have learned that republics are rarely lost in a single dramatic collapse, but surrendered in increments through fatigue, distraction, and the quiet normalization of the unacceptable. You have also learned that what is built through incremental surrender can be undone the same way—one refusal, one truth, one act of non-compliance at a time.

You have absorbed the lifecycle of the *Tyrannus Rex*. You have tracked the tactics of manipulation, mapped the mechanics of control, and seen how language is bent until it breaks. You now understand that the further a regime advances through the five stages, the more costly and dangerous resistance becomes. This knowledge is heavy. It strips away comforting illusions and reveals the political world as a ruthless battlefield of psychopaths and manipulation. That weight is real. I challenge you to carry it anyway. Awareness is not cynicism. It is clarity. And truth, however heavy, is the only armor that protects.

Authoritarian tactics depend on the predator understanding the prey better than the prey understands the predator. This book is an attempt to reverse that asymmetry.

History offers a lesson that despair often obscures: Apex predators go extinct. No regime is permanent. Ferdinand Marcos appeared immovable until citizens withdrew consent. The Soviet Union projected inevitability until its own internal contradictions collapsed it. Apartheid in South Africa was entrenched for generations until sustained civic resistance made it untenable. The pattern repeats. When citizens learn to see the system clearly, they refuse to internalize its narrative. They stop participating in their own diminution. The *Tyrannus Rex* feeds on compliance. Withhold it, and the predator starves.

Prebunking works only when it spreads. One inoculated mind is resilient, but a community of informed citizens is an immune system. Share the framework. Teach the patterns. Name the moves when you see them. Watch for early signs. Build relationships before they are urgently needed. Strengthen local institutions while they still function. Do not wait for a dramatic moment that signals it is "time" to act. Resilience is built long before the crisis peaks.

Most importantly, resist the lie of powerlessness. Authoritarian systems spend vast resources convincing citizens that resistance is futile precisely because they know it is not. You are not powerless. You are reading this. You are informed. And an informed citizen, anywhere in the world, is the thing the *Tyrannus Rex* fears most.

Selected Bibliography

INTRODUCTION

Prebunking

McGuire, W. J., & Papageorgis, D. (1961). The relative efficacy of various types of prior belief-defense in producing immunity against persuasion. *The Journal of Abnormal and Social Psychology*, 62(2), 327–337.

Purnat TD, Nguyen T, Briand S, editors. (2023). *Managing Infodemics in the 21st Century: Addressing New Public Health Challenges in the Information Ecosystem* [Internet]. Springer. PMID: 39556674.

van der Linden, S. (2024). *Foolproof: Why Misinformation Infects Our Minds and How to Build Immunity*. W. W. Norton & Company.

STAGE I: THE PATHOLOGIES OF POWER

Chaos Compulsion

Arceneaux, K., Gravelle, T. B., Osmundsen, M., Petersen, M. B., Reifler, J., & Scotto, T. J. (2021). Some People Just Want to Watch the World Burn: The Prevalence, Psychology, and Politics of the Need for Chaos. *Philosophical Transactions of the Royal Society B: Biological Sciences,* 376(1822), Article 20200147.

Cleckley, H. M. (1941/1988). *The Mask of Sanity: An Attempt to Clarify Some Issues About the So-called Psychopathic Personality* (5th ed.). Emily S. Cleckley.

Freud, S. (1920/1955). *Beyond the Pleasure Principle* (J. Strachey, Trans.). In J. Strachey (Ed.), *The Standard Edition of the Complete Psychological Works of Sigmund Freud* (Vol. 18, 7–64). Hogarth Press.

Fromm, E. (1973). *The Anatomy of Human Destructiveness*. Holt, Rinehart and Winston.

Edifice Complex

Boone, K., & Deming, M. E. (Eds.). (2024). *Empty Pedestals: Countering Confederate Narratives Through Public Design*. LSU Press.

French, H. W. (2017). *Everything Under the Heavens: How the Past Helps Shape China's Push for Global Power*. Alfred A. Knopf.

Lico, G. (2003). *Edifice Complex: Power, Myth, and Marcos State Architecture*. Ateneo de Manila University Press.

Nugent, W. (2008). *Habits of Empire: A History of American Expansionism*. Alfred A. Knopf.

Sudjic, D. (2005). *The Edifice Complex: How the Rich and Powerful Shape the World*. Penguin Press.

Grandiosity

Kernberg, O. F. (1975). *Borderline Conditions and Pathological Narcissism*. Jason Aronson.

O'Reilly, C. A., & Hall, N. (2021). Grandiose Narcissists and Decision Making: Impulsive, Overconfident, and Skeptical of Experts—But Seldom in Doubt. *Personality and Individual Differences*, 168, Article 110280.

Valachová, M., & Lisá, E. (2025). Narcissistic Grandiosity and Risky Behavior: Is There a Causal Effect? *SAGE Open*, 15(3).

Wink, P. (1991). Two Faces of Narcissism. *Journal of Personality and Social Psychology*, 61(4), 590–597.

Impunity Instinct

Eurasia Group & Kofi Annan Foundation. (2023). *The Atlas of Impunity*.

Furtado, H. T. (2022). *Politics of Impunity: Torture, the Armed Forces, and the Failure of Justice in Brazil*. Edinburgh University Press.

Haldemann, F., Unger, T., & Cadelo, V. (Eds.). (2018). *The United Nations Principles to Combat Impunity: A Commentary (Oxford Commentaries on International Law)*. Oxford University Press.

Nazareno, P. (2020). Impunity Reconsidered: International Law, Domestic Politics, and the Pursuit of Justice. *Harvard Human Rights Journal*, 33, 173–274.

Machiavellianism

Adorno, T. W., Frenkel-Brunswik, E., Levinson, D. J., & Sanford, R. N. (1950). *The Authoritarian Personality*. Harper & Brothers.

Christie, R., & Geis, F. (1970). *Studies in Machiavellianism*. Academic Press.

Machiavelli, N. (1532/2005). *The Prince* (P. Bondanella & M. Musa, Trans.). Oxford University Press.

Wilson, D. S., Near, D., & Miller, R. R. (1996). Machiavellianism: A Synthesis of the Evolutionary and Psychological Literatures. *Psychological Bulletin*, 119(2), 285–299.

Malignant Narcissism

Glad, B. (2002). Why Tyrants Go Too Far: Malignant Narcissism and Absolute Power. *Political Psychology*, 23(1), 1–37.

Post, J. M. (2004). *Leaders and Their Followers in a Dangerous World: The Psychology of Political Behavior*. Cornell University Press.

Post, J. M. (2015). *Narcissism and Politics: Dreams of Glory*. Cambridge University Press.

Vaknin, S. (2025). Narcissistic and Psychopathic Leaders. *Annals of Psychiatry and Treatment*, 9(1), 7–10.

Messianic Complex

Altemeyer, B. (2006). *The Authoritarians*. University of Manitoba.

Gorski, P. S., & Perry, S. L. (2022). *The Flag and the Cross: White Christian Nationalism and the Threat to American Democracy*. Oxford University Press.

Stewart, K. (2020). *The Power Worshippers: Inside the Dangerous Rise of Religious Nationalism*. Bloomsbury Publishing.

Yilmaz, I. (2021). *Creating the Desired Citizen: Ideology, State, and Islam in Turkey*. Cambridge University Press.

Predatory Kinship

Applebaum, A. (2024). Autocracy, Inc.: *The Dictators Who Want to Run the World*. Doubleday.

Levitsky, S., & Way, L. A. (2010). *Competitive Authoritarianism: Hybrid Regimes after the Cold War*. Cambridge University Press.

Naím, M. (2022). *The Revenge of Power: How Autocrats Are Reinventing Politics for the 21st Century*. St. Martin's Press.

Psychopathy

Babiak, P., & Hare, R. D. (2006). *Snakes in Suits: When Psychopaths Go to Work*. HarperCollins.

Boddy, C. R. (2011). *Corporate Psychopaths: Organisational Destructiveness*. Palgrave Macmillan.

Cleckley, H. M. (1941/1988). *The Mask of Sanity: An Attempt to Clarify Some Issues About the So-called Psychopathic Personality* (5th ed.). Emily S. Cleckley.

Dutton, K. (2012). *The Wisdom of Psychopaths: What Saints, Spies, and Serial Killers Can Teach Us About Success*. Scientific American / Farrar, Straus and Giroux.

Haycock, D. A. (2019). *Tyrannical Minds: Psychological Profiling, Narcissism, and Dictatorship*. Pegasus Books.

Sadism

Buckels, E. E., Jones, D. N., & Paulhus, D. L. (2013). Behavioral Confirmation of Everyday Sadism. *Psychological Science*, 24(11), 2201–2209.

Hershman, D. J., & Lieb, J. (1994). *A Brotherhood of Tyrants: Manic Depression and Absolute Power*. Prometheus Books.

Kurtulmuş, B. E. (2010). *The Dark Side of Leadership: An Institutional Perspective*. Palgrave Pivot.

Lobaczewski, A. M. (2006). *Political Ponerology: A Science on the Nature of Evil Adjusted for Political Purposes* (J. Reiss, Trans.; rev. ed.). Red Pill Press.

Snyder, T. (2010). *Bloodlands: Europe Between Hitler and Stalin*. Basic Books.

STAGE II: THE FABRICATION OF REALITY

Accusation in a Mirror

Burke, K. (1939). The rhetoric of Hitler's "Battle". *The Southern Review*, 5(1), 1–21.

Des Forges, A. L. (1999). *Leave None to Tell the Story: Genocide in Rwanda*. Human Rights Watch.

Stanton, G. H. (1996). *The Ten Stages of Genocide*. Genocide Watch.

Astroturfing

Bisnoff, J. (2019). *Fake Politics: How Corporate and Government Groups Create and Maintain a Monopoly on Truth*. Skyhorse Publishing.

Cialdini, R. B. (2021). *Influence, New and Expanded: The Psychology of Persuasion*. Harper Business.

King, G., Pan, J., & Roberts, M. E. (2017). How the Chinese Government Fabricates Social Media Posts for Strategic Distraction, Not Engaged Argument. *American Political Science Review*, 111(3), 484–501.

Walker, E. T. (2014). *Grassroots for Hire: Public Affairs Consultants in American Democracy*. Cambridge University Press.

Big Lie

Hitler, A. (1943/1944). *Mein Kampf* (R. Manheim, Trans.). Houghton Mifflin. (Original work published 1925–1926)

Kurlansky, M., & Zelz, E. (2022). *Big Lies: From Socrates to Social Media*. Tilbury House Publishers.

Langer, W. C. (1972). *The Mind of Adolf Hitler: The Secret Wartime Report*. Basic Books.

Lowenthal, L., & Guterman, N. (1949). *Prophets of Deceit: A Study of the Techniques of the American Agitator*. Harper & Brothers.

DARVO

Freyd, J. J. (1997). Violations of Power, Adaptive Blindness, and Betrayal Trauma Theory. *Feminism & Psychology*, 7(1), 22–32.

Freyd, J. J., & Birrell, P. J. (2013). *Blind to Betrayal: Why We Fool Ourselves We Aren't Being Fooled*. Trade Paper Press.

Harsey, S., & Freyd, J. J. (2020). Deny, Attack, and Reverse Victim and Offender (DARVO): What Is the Influence on Perceived Perpetrator and Victim Credibility? *Journal of Aggression, Maltreatment & Trauma*, 29(8), 897–916.

Mirza, D. (2019). *The Covert Passive-Aggressive Narcissist*. Debbie Mirza Coaching.

Noor, M., Shnabel, N., Halabi, S., & Nadler, A. (2012). The Psychology of Competitive Victimhood in Violent Conflicts. *Psychological Bulletin*, 138(3), 351–374.

Firehose of Falsehood

Jankowicz, N. (2021). *How to Lose the Information War: Russia, Fake News, and the Future of Conflict*. I. B. Tauris.

Kanefield, T., & Dorian, P. (2024). *A Firehose of Falsehood: The Story of Disinformation* (Hardcover ed.). World Citizen Comics.

Paul, C., & Matthews, M. (2016). *The Russian "Firehose of Falsehood" Propaganda Model: Why It Might Work and Options to Counter It*. RAND Corporation.

Gaslighting

Arendt, H. (1951). *The Origins of Totalitarianism*. Schocken Books.

Stanley, J. (2018). *How Propaganda Works*. Princeton University Press.

Stern, R. (2007). *The Gaslight Effect: How to Spot and Survive the Hidden Manipulation Others Use to Control Your Life*. Morgan Road Books.

Media Capture

Dragomir, M. (2019). *Media Capture in Europe*. Center for Media, Data and Society.

Guriev, S., & Treisman, D. (2019). Informational Autocrats. *American Political Science Review*, 33(4), 100–127.

Pomerantsev, P. (2015). *Nothing is True and Everything is Possible: The Surreal Heart of the New Russia*. PublicAffairs.

Schiffrin, A. (Ed.). (2021). *Media Capture: How Money, Digital Platforms, and Governments Control the News*. Columbia University Press.

Newspeak

Klemperer, V. (2000). *LTI: Lingua Tertii Imperii—A Philologist's Notebook* (M. B. Herring, Trans.). Continuum. (Original work published 1947).

Orwell, G. (1949/2021). *Nineteen Eighty-Four*. Penguin Classics.

Young, J. W. (1991). *Totalitarian language: Orwell's Newspeak and its Nazi and Communist antecedents*. University Press of Virginia.

Rewriting History

Stanley, J. (2024). *Erasing History: How Fascists Rewrite the Past to Control the Future*. Simon & Schuster.

Szafonova, T. (Ed.). (2025). Paradoxes of historical revisionism in the authoritarian states [Special Issue]. *Journal of Contemporary Central and Eastern Europe*, 33(2). Taylor & Francis Online.

Trouillot, M.-R. (1995). *Silencing the Past: Power and the Production of History*. Beacon Press.

War on Expertise

Mann, M. E. & Hotez, P. J. (2025). *Science Under Siege: How to Fight the Five Most Powerful Forces that Threaten Our World*. PublicAffairs.

McIntyre, L. (2018). *Post-truth*. MIT Press.

Nichols, T. (2017). *The Death of Expertise: The Campaign Against Established Knowledge and Why It Matters*. Oxford University Press.

Oreskes, N., & Conway, E. M. (2010). *Merchants of Doubt: How a Handful of Scientists Obscured the Truth on Issues from Tobacco Smoke to Global Warming*. Bloomsbury Press.

STAGE III: THE MECHANICS OF CONTROL

Apathy Trap

Applebaum, A. (2021). *Twilight of Democracy: The Seductive Lure of Authoritarianism*. Vintage.

Kendzior, S. (2020). *Hiding in Plain Sight: The Invention of Donald Trump and the Erosion of America*. Flatiron Books.

Seligman, M. E. P. (1975). *Helplessness: On Depression, Development, and Death*. W.H. Freeman.

Sunstein, C. R. (2022). *Sludge: What Stops Us from Getting Things Done and What to Do about It*. MIT Press.

Atomization

Chan, A. T. (2025). *Beyond Coercion: The Politics of Inequality in China*. Cambridge University Press.

Kornhauser, W. (1959/2008). *The Politics of Mass Society*. Routledge.

Putnam, R. D. (2020). *Bowling Alone: Revised and Updated—The Collapse and Revival of American Community* (Revised & updated ed.). Simon & Schuster.

Bread and Circuses

Guriev, S., & Treisman, D. (2022). *Spin Dictators: The Changing Face of Tyranny in the 21st Century*. Princeton University Press.

Human Rights Foundation. (2024). *Sports and Dictators: A History of Sports & Dictators Series*. Human Rights Foundation.

Muhtadi, B. (2019). *Vote Buying in Indonesia: The Mechanics of Institutional Systematic Fraud*. Palgrave Macmillan.

Zimbalist, A. (2015). *Circus Maximus: The Economic Gamble Behind Hosting the Olympics and the World Cup*. Brookings Institution Press.

Coded Signaling

López, I. H. (2014). *Dog Whistle Politics: How Coded Racial Appeals Have Reinvented Racism and Wrecked the Middle Class*. Oxford University Press.

López, I. H. (2019). *Merge Left: Fusing Race and Class, Winning Elections, and Saving America*. The New Press.

Saul, J. M. (2024). *Dogwhistles and Figleaves: How Manipulative Language Spreads Racism and Falsehood*. Oxford University Press.

Demonization

Haslam, N. (2006). Dehumanization: An Integrative Review. *Personality and Social Psychology Review*, 10(3), 252–264.

Keen, S. (1986). *Faces of the Enemy: Reflections of the Hostile Imagination*. Harper & Row.

Smith, D. L. (2011). *Less Than Human: Why We Demean, Enslave, and Exterminate Others*. St. Martin's Press.

Straus, S. (2008). *The Order of Genocide: Race, Power, and War in Rwanda*. Cornell University Press.

Diversionary War

Levy, J. S. (1989). The diversionary theory of war: A critique. In M. I. Midlarsky (Ed.), *Handbook of War Studies* (259–288). Unwin Hyman.

Maddox, J. D. (2016). How to Start a War: Eight Cases of Strategic Provocation. *Narrative and Conflict: Explorations in Theory and Practice*, 3(1), 66–109.

Mueller, J. (1970). Presidential Popularity from Truman to Johnson. *The American Political Science Review*, 64(1), 18–34.

Oakes, A. (2012). *Diversionary War: Domestic Unrest and International Conflict*. Stanford University Press.

Foreign Agent Trap

Chaudhry, S. (2022). The Assault on Civil Society: Explaining State Crackdown on NGOs. *International Organization*, 76(3), 549–590.

Flikke, G. (2016). Resurgent Authoritarianism: The Case of Russia's New NGO Law. *Post-Soviet Affairs*, 32(2), 103–131.

Keck, M. E., & Sikkink, K. (1998). *Activists Beyond Borders: Advocacy Networks in International Politics*. Cornell University Press.

Informant Systems

Blaydes, L. (2018). *State of Repression: Iraq Under Saddam Hussein*. Princeton University Press.

Dennis, M., & Laporte, N. (2014). *The Stasi: Myth and Reality*. Routledge.

Dimitrov, M. K. (2022). *Dictatorship and Information: Authoritarian Regime Resilience in Communist Europe and China*. Oxford University Press.

Gause, K. E. (2012). *Coercion, Control, Surveillance, and Punishment: An Examination of the North Korean Police State*. Committee for Human Rights in North Korea.

Panopticon

Greenwald, G. (2014). *No Place to Hide: Edward Snowden, the NSA, and the U.S. Surveillance State*. Metropolitan Books.

Pei, M. (2024). *The Sentinel State: Surveillance and the Survival of Dictatorship in China*. Harvard University Press.

Richard, L., & Rigaud, S. (2023). *Pegasus: How a Spy in Your Pocket Threatens the End of Privacy, Dignity, and Democracy*. Henry Holt and Co.

Zuboff, S. (2019). *The Age of Surveillance Capitalism: The Fight for a Human Future at the New Frontier of Power*. PublicAffairs.

Scapegoating

Allport, G. W. (1954/1979). *The Nature of Prejudice*. Addison-Wesley. Basic Books.

Douglas, T. (1995). *Scapegoats: Transferring Blame*. Routledge.

Glick, P. (2002). Sacrificial Lambs Dressed in Wolves' Clothing: Envious Prejudice, Ideology, and the Scapegoating of Jews. In L. S. Newman & R. Erber (Eds.), *Understanding Genocide: The Social Psychology of the Holocaust* (113–142). Oxford University Press.

Milburn, M. A., & Conrad, S. D. (2016). *Raised to Rage: The Politics of Anger and the Roots of Authoritarianism*. MIT Press.

STAGE IV: THE THEATER OF DEMOCRACY

Constitutional Vandalism

Ginsburg, T., & Huq, A. Z. (2018). *How to Save a Constitutional Democracy*. University of Chicago Press.

Levitsky, S., & Ziblatt, D. (2018). *How Democracies Die*. Crown.

Scheppele, K. L. (2018). Autocratic Legalism. *University of Chicago Law Review*, 85(2), 545–583.

Varol, O. O. (2015). Stealth Authoritarianism. *Iowa Law Review*, 100(4), 1673–1742.

Controlled Opposition

Gandhi, J. (2010). *Political Institutions Under Dictatorship*. Cambridge University Press.

Magaloni, B. (2006). *Voting for Autocracy: Hegemonic Party Survival in Mexico*. Cambridge University Press.

Schedler, A. (Ed.). (2006). *Electoral Authoritarianism: The Dynamics of Unfree Competition*. Lynne Rienner Publishers.

Schedler, A. (2013). *The Politics of Uncertainty: Sustaining and Subverting Electoral Authoritarianism*. Oxford University Press.

Crony Capitalism

Bueno de Mesquita, B., & Smith, A. (2011). *The Dictator's Handbook: Why Bad Behavior is Almost Always Good Politics*. PublicAffairs.

Bullough, O. (2019). *Moneyland: The Inside Story of the Crooks and Kleptocrats Who Rule the World*. St. Martin's Press.

Dawisha, K. (2014). *Putin's Kleptocracy: Who Owns Russia?* Simon & Schuster.

Pei, M. (2016). *China's Crony Capitalism: The Dynamics of Regime Decay*. Harvard University Press.

Faux Elections

Bunce, V. J., & Wolchik, S. L. (2012). *Defeating Authoritarian Leaders in Postcommunist Countries*. Cambridge University Press.

Chenoweth, E., & Stephan, M. J. (2011). *Why Civil Resistance Works: The Strategic Logic of Nonviolent Conflict*. Columbia University Press.

Westminster Foundation for Democracy. (2025, June 6). *Understanding Parallel Vote Tabulation: An Explainer for International Partners*. Westminster Foundation for Democracy.

Institutional Capture

Bermeo, N. (2016). On democratic backsliding. *Journal of Democracy*, 27(1), 5–19.

Levitsky, S., & Ziblatt, D. (2018). *How Democracies Die*. Crown.

Müller, J.-W. (2016). *What Is Populism?* University of Pennsylvania Press.

Lawfare

Ginsburg, T., & Moustafa, T. (Eds.). (2008). *Rule by Law: The Politics of Courts in Authoritarian Regimes*. Cambridge University Press.

Kittrie, O. F. (2016). *Lawfare: Law as a Weapon of War*. Oxford University Press.
Scheppele, K. L. (2018). Autocratic Legalism. *The University of Chicago Law Review*, 85(2), 545–583.

Performative Leadership

Dunbar, E. (2024). *The Psychology of Authoritarian Leaders: Strongmen, Crooks, and Celebrities*. Springer

Francois, P., Rainer, I., & Trebbi, F. (2014). The Dictator's Inner Circle (NBER Working Paper No. 20216). *National Bureau of Economic Research*.

Lalancette, M., & Raynauld, V. (2017). The Power of Political Image: Justin Trudeau, Instagram, and Celebrity Politics. *American Behavioral Scientist*, 63(7), 888–924.

Pomerantsev, P. (2020). *This is Not Propaganda: Adventures in the War Against Reality*. Faber and Faber.

Salami Tactics

Ginsburg, T. & Huq, A. (2018). *How to Save a Constitutional Democracy*. University of Chicago Press.

Hostovsky Brandes, T., & Roznai, Y. (2024). When the first brick falls of the fortress of democracy: Dealing with the first slice of the 'salami tactic' for eroding democracy. *Asian Journal of Comparative Law*, 19(3), 535–555.

Schelling, T. C. (1966). *Arms and influence*. Yale University Press.

Self-Coup

Call, C. (2021, January 8). *No, it's not a coup. It's a failed self-coup that will undermine U.S. leadership and democracy worldwide*. Brookings Institution.

Goldsmith, A. A. (2024). Power grabs from the top: A database of self-coups. *International Studies Quarterly*, 68(4), sqae147. https://doi.org/10.1093/isq/sqae147

Hemel, D. J. (2022). Self-coup and the constitution. *Constitutional Commentary*, 37(3), 315–329.

Luttwak, E. N. (2016). *Coup d'état: A Practical Handbook* (Revised ed.). Harvard University Press.

State of Exception

Agamben, G. (2005). *State of Exception* (K. Attell, Trans.). University of Chicago Press.

Cercel, C., Fusco, G.-G., & Lavis, S. (Eds.). (2022). *States of Exception: Law, History, Theory*. Routledge.

Dyzenhaus, D. (2006). *The Constitution of Law: Legality in a Time of Emergency*. Cambridge University Press.

Gerstle, G., & Isaac, J. (Eds.). (2020). *States of Exception in American History*. Cambridge University Press.

Schmitt, C. (2005). *Political Theology: Four Chapters on the Concept of Sovereignty* (G. Schwab, Trans.). University of Chicago Press.

STAGE V: THE STATE OF TERROR

Agents Provocateurs

Cunningham, D. (2004). *There's Something Happening Here: The New Left, the Klan, and FBI Counterintelligence*. University of California Press.

Marx, G. T. (1974). Thoughts on a neglected category of social movement participant: The agent provocateur and the informant. *American Journal of Sociology*, 80(2), 402–442.

Marx, G. T. (1988). *Undercover: Police Surveillance in Comparative Perspective*. University of California Press.

Pentney, K. (2021). Licensed to kill...discourse? agents provocateurs and a purposive right to freedom of expression. *Netherlands Quarterly of Human Rights*, 39(3), 241–257.

Williams, K. (2015). *Witness to Betrayal: Profiles of Provocateurs*. Emergency Hearts Publishing.

Brownshirts

Mahony, L., & Eguren, L. E. (1997). *Unarmed Bodyguards: International Accompaniment for the Protection of Human Rights*. Kumarian Press.

Sharp, G. (1973). *The Politics of Nonviolent Action (Parts 1–3)*. Porter Sargent Publisher.

Siemens, D. (2017). *Stormtroopers: A New History of Hitler's Brownshirts*. Yale University Press.

Collective Punishment

Alexopoulos, G. (2008). Stalin and the Politics of Kinship: Practices of Collective Punishment, 1920s–1940s. *Comparative Studies in Society and History*, 50(1), 91–117.

Dukalskis, A. (2021). *Making the World Safe for Dictatorship: Peer Surveillance and Transnational Repression*. Oxford University Press.

Hawk, D. R., & Committee for Human Rights in North Korea. (2012). *The Hidden Gulag: The Lives and Voices of "Those who are sent to the mountains"* (2nd ed.). U.S. Committee for Human Rights in North Korea.

Enforced Disappearance

CONADEP (National Commission on the Disappearance of Persons). (1984). *Nunca Más (Never Again)*. Eudeba.

Feitlowitz, M. (1998). *A Lexicon of Terror: Argentina and the Legacies of Torture*. Oxford University Press.

Heath, J., & Zahedi, A. (Eds.). (2023). *Book of the Disappeared: The Quest for Transnational Justice*. University of Michigan Press.

Scovazzi, T., & Citroni, G. (2007). *The Struggle Against Enforced Disappearance and the 2007 United Nations Convention*. Martinus Nijhoff Publishers.

False Flags

Fantina, R., & Sheehan, C. (2020). *Propaganda, Lies, and False Flags: How the U.S. Justifies its Wars*. Clarity Press.

Ganser, D. (2005). *NATO's Secret Armies: Operation GLADIO and Terrorism in Western Europe*. Frank Cass.

Hett, B. C. (2014). *Burning the Reichstag: An Investigation Into the Third Reich's Enduring Mystery*. Oxford University Press.

Hughes, G. (2011). *The Military's Role in Counterterrorism: Examples and Implications for Liberal Democracies*. U.S. Army War College Press.

Joint Chiefs of Staff. (1962). Justification for U.S. Military Intervention in Cuba (Operation Northwoods). Top Secret Memorandum. [Declassified].

Snyder, T. (2017). *On Tyranny: Twenty Lessons from the Twentieth Century*. Crown.

Kompromat

Ioffe, J. (Jan. 11, 2017). How State-Sponsored Blackmail Works in Russia. *The Atlantic*.

Ledeneva, A. V. (2006). *How Russia Really Works: The Informal Practices that Shaped Post-Soviet Politics and Business*. Cornell University Press.

Oates, S. (2017). Kompromat goes global?: Assessing a Russian media tool in the United States. *Slavic Review*, 76(S1), S57–S65.

Mass Detention

Applebaum, A. (2003). *Gulag: A History*. Anchor Books.

Maddow, R. (Host). (2025). *Rachel Maddow presents: Burn order* [Audio podcast]. MSNBC.

Roberts, S. R. (2020). *The War on the Uyghurs: China's Internal Campaign Against a Muslim Minority*. Princeton University Press.

Solzhenitsyn, A. I. (1973). *The Gulag Archipelago*, 1918–1956. Harper & Row.

Pacification

Coyne, C. J., & Hall, A. R. (2018). *Tyranny Comes Home: The Domestic Fate of U.S. Militarism*. Stanford University Press.

Graham, S. (2010). *Cities Under Siege: The New Military Urbanism*. Verso.

Halper, J. (2015). *War Against the People: Israel, the Palestinians and Global Pacification*. Pluto Press.

McQuade, B. (2019). *Pacifying the Homeland: Intelligence Fusion and Mass Supervision*. University of California Press.

Political Purges

Brzezinski, Z. (1956). *The Permanent Purge: Politics in Soviet Totalitarianism*. Harvard University Press.

Getty, J. A., & Naumov, O. V. (1999). *The Road to Terror: Stalin and the Self-Destruction of the Bolsheviks*, 1932–1939. Yale University Press.

Svolik, M. W. (2012). *The Politics of Authoritarian Rule*. Cambridge University Press.

Spectacle Executions

Blake, H. (2019). *From Russia with Blood: The Kremlin's Ruthless Assassination Program and Vladimir Putin's Secret War on the West*. Mulholland Books.

Callamard, A. (2019). *Annex to the Report of the Special Rapporteur on extrajudicial, summary or arbitrary executions: Investigation into the unlawful death of Mr. Jamal Khashoggi*. United Nations Human Rights Council.

Cooley, A., & Heathershaw, J. (2017). *Dictators Without Borders: Power and Money in Central Asia*. Yale University Press.

Schenkkan, N., & Linzer, I. (2021). *Out of Sight, Not Out of Reach: The Global Scale of Transnational Repression*. Freedom House.

About the Author

E.A. Blair has spent a career studying how influence works—in organizations, in media, and in the hands of those who abuse it. That expertise was for hire for many years, its levers pulled in the service of corporations and government agencies seeking to shape behavior at scale. This book is the other side of that ledger. Blair finally decided to show everyone what and where the levers are.

A *Tyrannus Rex* can survive hatred.
It cannot survive laughter.

Report for duty at:
www.tyrannusrex.com

www.ingramcontent.com/pod-product-compliance
Lightning Source LLC
LaVergne TN
LVHW010850240726
843924LV00044B/270
* 9 7 9 8 9 9 5 4 4 2 5 0 9 *